Don't Get Married Until You Read This

A Layman's Guide to Prenuptial Agreements

David Saltman, J.D., L.L.M.
Harry Schaffner, J.D.

BARRON'S

New York • London • Toronto • Sydney

All inquiries should be addressed to:
Barron's Educational Series, Inc.
250 Wireless Boulevard
Hauppauge, New York 11788

International Standard Book No. 0-8120-4123-2

Library of Congress Catalog Card No. 89–67

Library of Congress Cataloging in Publication Data

Saltman, David A.
    Don't get married until you read this: a layman's guide to
prenuptial agreements/David Saltman.
    p.   cm.
    Includes index.
    ISBN 0-8120-4123-2
1. Antenuptial contracts—United States—Popular works.
I. Schaffner, Harry II. Title.
KF529.Z9S25   1989
346.7301'6—dc 19
[347.30616]   89-67

PRINTED IN THE UNITED STATES OF AMERICA

901 800 0987654321

Dedication

This book is dedicated to my partner for life, Robin .

David Saltman

To my mother, Tillie Schaffner, who knows more about marriage and family than anyone.

Harry Schaffner

Table of Contents

Acknowledgments

I wish to thank and acknowledge Grace Freedson and Carolyn Horne of Barron's for their faith in me concerning this project; Julie Blitzer, Esq., for her substantial contributions; James Stahl, Esq., for his encouragement and faith; Richard Altman, Esq., for his care and encouragement and friendship of 15 years; Cindy Van Hise for her friendship, constructive criticism, and endless hours of typing and help; and also my children, Kari, Andy, Jason, and Julie for the lessons that they have given me about what is really important in life.

I also wish to thank John Martin of Matthew Bender, Matthew Bender itself for allowing me to use my previous works, and Adele Lewis and Bill Lewis for their encouragement at the beginning of my writing career.

—David Saltman

Many thoughts of appreciation to Colette Anderson, J.D., my partner; Carole Dickerson and Liz Malette, my secretaries; and especially my wife, Ann, and my daughters Liza, Jennifer, and Dana.

—Harry Schaffner

About the Authors

Mr. Saltman is a 1972 graduate of the Dickinson School of Law, where he received a J.D. degree, and a 1983 graduate of New York University Law School, where he received an LL.M. degree. He has written previous articles and chapters on prenuptial agreements, is the author of numerous other articles relating to divorce and trial advocacy, and co-author of *Layman's Guide to Legal Survival*. He practices in East Windsor, New Jersey, a small town outside of Princeton.

Mr. Schaffner is a 1966 graduate of the University of Illinois College of Law. He specializes in family law, is a fellow of the American Academy of Matrimonial Lawyers, The Executive Committee on Property and Maintenance of the American Bar Association's Family Law Section, and is a frequent lecturer at continuing education seminars for lawyers. He practices in Dundee, Illinois, a suburb of Chicago.

Preface

Most people use a lawyer when buying a house. "After all," they reason, "it's the biggest purchase of our lives." Yet most people know very little about their legal rights before marriage. It is a time of romance and happiness. The sterile, formal interior of a lawyer's office seems hardly the setting for a couple filled with happiness, dreams, and hope.

The wealthy often have involved a lawyer in the process of marriage and estate planning before marriage. Each of us is wealthy to the extent of our own wealth. Without going to a lawyer and asking, "What are my rights?" this book can help you privately explore your legal rights and options for yourself through the experience and advice of two specialists in premarital agreements.

Like most of the law, marriage law differs from state to state. General principles that seem to apply to most states' laws are discussed here. The names of people in the case studies have been changed to protect their identities. Their problems are real and the solutions they or a court reached are likewise real.

No one should get married without a better understanding of his or her legal rights and duties. We require young people to take driver's education courses and we test everyone before they can have a driver's license, yet, there is no test of your knowledge before marriage.

This book will provide you with the information you need to make intelligent choices about your property and income so that there will be a lasting and permanent benefit to you.

FOR STARTERS . . .

CHAPTER 1
Background

The basic concept of the prenuptial agreement has been around for hundreds of years. Betrothal contracts, a very close cousin to modern prenuptial agreements, were commonplace among the royalty of Old England. Marriage arrangements, which included provisions for the ownership and distribution of property, were executed by a guardian within a matter of months of an infant's birth. These arrangements were cause for great celebration.

Today the majority of marriages is still arranged. India with 700 million people and China with over 1 billion people still practice arranged marriages.

If a young man in the central African country of Rowanda, the most densely populated country on earth, sees a girl he likes and is interested in marriage, he must tell his father who will discuss it with her father. If agreed upon, there must be the payment of one cow from the groom's family to the bride's family and the marriage is then arranged.

The romantic courtship did not arrive in western countries until the twentieth century. It is a process of mate selection that permits the two prospective married people to decide on their own to get married, and is but a fleeting experiment.

During the first half of the twentieth century, Jews and Orientals lived in tightly confined neighborhoods in our cities. Mate selection, although not openly arranged, came as a product of a highly complex social structure involving deep ethnic and national origins, money, education, and length of time in America. Jews and Orientals had divorce rates that were much lower than the U.S. average. Until

1960, those rates were under 5 percent. This gave rise to the saying: "Jewish men make the best husbands."

As ghettos dissolved, Americanization took over and romantic courtship began to take the form of the rest of America. So did the divorce rate. The Oriental-American divorce rate, once under 3 percent, now approaches the unfortunate national average. The Jewish divorce rate once exceedingly low, now equals or exceeds the national average.

In other parts of the world, romantic courtship has also become the norm. In Japan, where arranged marriages had been the centuries-old tradition, the DeBeers diamond cartel (whose advertising slogan has been "Diamonds are Forever" since the early thirties) began in the 1970s to advertise its diamond rings. Ads with young couples in western clothing, courting and swooning over a diamond engagement ring, were placed in Japanese magazines. The result: romantic courtship has become the norm in the major cities, such as Tokyo and Kyoto, and the divorce rate approaches western countries.

Interfaith marriage also has become more prevalent. Among Jews, for example, one third marrying for the first time and 70 percent marrying for the second time marry a non-Jew. Pasta has joined pirogies, bagels, and paprikash on family tables. "Seasons greetings" or "happy holidays" has become the common December greeting. There now are a sufficient number of clergy who are willing to perform interfaith marriages; a religious ceremony without formal conversion generally is possible.

The U.S. Department of Health and Human Services gathers statistics from the various state agencies on birth and divorce rates. Statistics about how we live are gathered and analyzed by special statisticians called demographers. They have shown that, roughly speaking, in the urban areas of the country—New York, Chicago, Dallas, Los Angeles, for example—the divorce rate exceeds 50 percent. In most large cities and their sprawling suburbs, there are more divorces each year than the number of marriage certificates issued by that county. If you look closely, you will see that for people who have been married before, the divorce rate is even higher.

In 1987, in one-third of all couples getting married at least one of them had been married before. In fact, in 20 percent of all marriages both the bride and groom had been married before.

Many, many people are now marrying much later with significant assets that they are not always willing to relinquish. In addition, many married women have chosen to work outside the home, even after children are born. These women are acquiring and managing their own personal assets. Couples are also bringing children into the second marriages.

These new marriages are much more complex than those of a young married couple. It is easy to see why today's couples are realizing that they must protect their interests.

CHAPTER 2
The Built-in Laws

What Is Equitable Distribution?

In the early 1970s, the Uniform Laws Commission, a private, nonprofit organization made up of some of the brightest law professors and lawyers, turned its attention to the patchwork quilt of family law. This organization had been successful in having every state adopt the Uniform Commercial Code, which permits commerce among the businesses of America without regard to any peculiar local law of a particular place.

The Uniform Marriage and Dissolution of Marriage Act is such a law and has been passed by four state legislatures. It introduced a concept called "equitable distribution." Under equitable distribution, all property acquired during the marriage is "marital property" and all property owned before the marriage is "nonmarital property." Also, a gift or inheritance to either spouse during the marriage is nonmarital property.

Equitable distribution views marriage as a partnership and attempts to equalize the roles of men and women by viewing the contributions of a homemaker and caretaking parent as every bit as important as the contributions of the spouse in the business world.

Roger and Marilyn were married for 19 years. Marilyn was the traditional homemaker and caretaker of the three children born during the marriage. Roger began a telephone answering business, which he incorporated and purchased stock entirely in his own name. He went into pagers when they were introduced, and then he bought two cellular car phone systems in midwestern cities when they became available from the federal government. He worked extraordinary hours and was seldom home.

Marilyn filed suit for divorce because of her sense that this was "no marriage." The law in this equitable distribution state viewed the $18 million business empire as marital property and Marilyn's homemaker role as equally important.

The following states are equitable distribution states, by either statute or case decision: Alabama, Alaska, Arizona, Arkansas, California, Colorado, Connecticut, Delaware, District of Columbia, Florida, Hawaii, Idaho, Illinois, Indiana, Iowa, Kansas, Kentucky, Louisiana, Maine, Massachusetts, Michigan, Minnesota, Missouri, Montana, Nebraska, Nevada, New Hampshire, New Jersey, New Mexico, New York, North Carolina, North Dakota, Oklahoma, Oregon, Pennsylvania, Rhode Island, South Dakota, Tennessee, Texas, Utah, Vermont, Washington, Wisconsin, Wyoming.

In an equitable distribution state, the court must "equitably divide" (not necessarily "equally divide") the marital property. The court in an equitable distribution state should consider the length of the marriage; age, health, occupation, skills, and employment of the parties; custodial provisions for children; and value of the property. Many arguments over the value of property are likely to occur. Remember, equitable division does not necessarily mean equal division.

Community Property States

Primarily because of historical origins, eight states are community property states: Arizona, California, Idaho, Louisiana, Nevada, New Mexico, Texas and Washington.

In community property states, there must be an equal (one-half) division of the community property in the event of divorce. California has brought us much litigation involving entertainment personalities who attempt to protect their present and future acquired assets from the one-half division of property required in a divorce in a community property state.

Why Have A Prenuptial Agreement if the Law Is What It Is?

If in an equitable distribution state the law separates to each spouse all their premarriage assets, isn't that essentially a prenuptial agreement that typically provides that each spouse has what is his or hers before the marriage?

For 14 years, Sandra worked at her husband's grain elevator, which he owned before the marriage. It was a corporation and he owned all the stock. She worked without pay, except that, after the IRA rules were introduced, he paid her enough to make an IRA contribution. Although he told her that he put her name on the family checking account, it was only printed on the checks, but he never turned the signature card in to the bank. The bank required that Sandra personally guaranty, with Bob, the line of credit business loan. Bob and Sandra ran much of their personal expenses through the business. All the cars were owned by the company and even a very expensive motor home used for pleasure was a business asset. A swimming pool installed at Bob's house owned before the marriage was paid for by the business.

When Bob and Sandra got divorced, the court said that Bob's company was still his. However, the labor and efforts made by Sandra, which helped his business grow, were a marital contribution to his nonmarital company for which she must be reimbursed. The cars, swimming pool, and motor home, personal items that Bob was hiding in his company, were to be considered marital property.

Things can be rather confusing if left up to the law. Is it marital property or was the house bought "in contemplation" of marriage?

Is a gift of $10,000 made to both husband and wife or just wife from her parents, if it was at an anniversary party and before the whole family (the check made payable to wife only)?

"The only reason I put the house in joint tenancy is that the lady at the bank told me I had to because I'm married," is a story heard every day in divorce lawyers' offices.

A prenuptial agreement would have specified exactly how Bob and Sandra could have split their assets and avoided a number of problems. It could decide who would receive the $10,000 gift and who would get the house. And it could be done outside of a divorce court.

Prenuptial agreements are becoming more and more popular in American society today. As the popularity of these agreements increases, states have began to provide rules and statutes for their establishment and enforceability. The law in this area is still relatively new compared to other types of contract law. It is rapidly evolving.

Summary

In the absence of a prenuptial agreement, the laws of each state automatically provide for a method of distributing marital property. A prenuptial agreement, however, is a way the parties rather than the state, can decide how property will be distributed.

CHAPTER 3
The Prenuptial Agreement

The Short Definition

A prenuptial agreement is a written contract between a man and woman entered into before marriage. It changes the way the law would normally deal with their property, income, and responsibilities to each other when their marriage ends by death or divorce. (After all, *all* marriages end one way or the other.) Prenuptial agreements are sometimes called antenuptial agreements (from the Latin prefix "ante," which means before, and "nuptial," which means marriage) and sometimes called premarital agreements.

Historical Background

Like much else about the law, some understanding of historical context is helpful. You need not be a historian to understand it. Everyone knows that an agreement to buy or sell land must be in writing. Many people know that an agreement to pay the debt of another person must be in writing. Those rules come from an ancient law, the Statute of Frauds. It is a written law in some form or other in every state. It is a direct descendant of English law and each state upon adopting their earliest laws passed a Statute of Frauds.

In an unusual mood of charity, Sam told his future son-in-law, Harold, that after Harold married his daughter, Sam would give Harold a job and half the stock in his company. After the

11

marriage, Sam quickly became doubtful about Harold and Harold's motives for marriage. Sam's promise is unenforceable.

A verbal agreement in which marriage is the promise of one person in exchange for something of value from the other is not legally binding because it is oral, not written.

There was a time when no prenuptial agreement was legally enforceable. It was said to be "against public policy," which is lawyer shorthand for generally unstated principles of fairness. The law was not going to allow people to dictate what would become of their property upon divorce.

The Modern Trend

Every state, to some extent, permits prenuptial agreements. The trend in the law was led by Florida, where marriages among widowed people are common, in a case that held that a written contract between two people before marriage is binding and legally enforceable. This landmark decision in the United States held that prenuptial agreements are not "against public policy." Today most states have statutes that specifically permit prenuptial contracts. Arizona and California, retirement states as well, have also led in the development of the law.

There are many types of prenuptial agreements. Each one can be custom-tailored to suit the requirements of the particular relationship. By reading the case histories in this book you will probably find a situation similar to your own and learn which sample paragraphs are relevant to your situation.

Most people want to avoid having a divorce court decide how to divide the assets they have accumulated or will accumulate. They don't want a third party deciding their future and don't want to pay extra legal fees. They want to avoid the anxiety, frustration, and emotional disruption of coming to a financial agreement in the midst of divorce, and have chosen to define their assets so there will be no misunderstanding.

Keeping Prior Assets Separate

George and Ava's marriage was the culmination of many sessions with lawyers. Each had been married before and

George had a thriving business, grown children, and show horses. The prenuptial agreement had a schedule of George's assets and Ava's (she had a short list). If the marriage ended in divorce (which it predictably did), Ava received $100,000, no alimony or maintenance, and no interest in the business, the residence, or the show horses.

George and Ava's agreement changed the law. Otherwise, in a divorce settlement Ava might have received millions of dollars and at least one residence.

Prenuptial agreements may be used to keep each party's assets completely separate. This type of agreement releases each person's rights to the other's assets on death, separation, or dissolution of the marriage. It normally covers any and all property obtained before or during the marriage.

A prenuptial agreement may be in the best interest of a couple who are both reasonably wealthy and do not need to rely upon each other for financial support, but are marrying more for companionship. If one or both spouses has accumulated a significant amount of wealth or has children from a prior marriage, an agreement may be appropriate. In this scenario, the couple may wish to share in all assets that are accumulated during the marriage and keep separate and apart those accumulated prior to marriage. For example, if a partner owns a small business or closely-related family corporation and wants to keep its assets intact should a divorce occur, a prenuptial agreement is a good idea. If children from a previous marriage are involved and the parent wants them to benefit from their wealth, an agreement is in order.

Providing Financial Security for Spouse or Children

A person with less wealth may gain financial security without giving up assets. One of the parties not only may have accumulated substantial assets prior to the relationship, but also may have children for whom he or she wishes to inherit the majority of the wealth. The prenuptial agreement may guarantee the spouse a fixed amount of money or property upon separation, divorce, or death. In this instance, both parties will be secure in the event the marriage ends unexpectedly. The remaining spouse will have enough money to maintain a reasonable life-style. At the same time, the wealthier spouse knows that no claim against the estate will be made and that assets will pass to the children without any problems.

Insuring Religious Practice

Bob was Jewish and Carol, Catholic. Bob's ties to his family were so great that Carol converted to Judaism. They had two children. In the divorce, Carol agreed to continue the Jewish education of the children even though she had custody. But Carol returned to her church after a time, and wanted the children to appreciate both religions and cultures. Bob took Carol back to court to have her held in contempt. A judge had the difficult task of enforcing an agreement about religion (not a traditional subject for American courts). Carol was ordered to continue the children's Jewish training or be jailed for contempt.

Religion is a very sensitive issue with many people and therefore deep thought and thorough discussion should be given to the religious training of his children, her children, and our children. Considerations must be made as to current religious upbringing and to what will happen in the event of death of a parent. Remember, too, that not all states enforce religious upbringing in the same way— the facts of each case and laws of each state are determinants.

Thorough and final discussions about religion should begin early in any conversation about a prenuptial agreement. Intermarriage, as well as marriage within different groups of a single faith, can have many unforeseen difficulties. As many of these difficulties as possible should be elicited early in your relationship.

Treating Everyone Fairly

In nearly all states, the law requires both parties to disclose all relevant information before a prenuptial agreement can be signed and viewed as valid. This requirement does not exist in the same degree in an ordinary business contract. A prenuptial agreement is personal in nature, and so the law requires and demands that each party deal honestly, openly, and fairly with the other and disclose all assets and debts.

This does not mean that you cannot prevent your spouse from having certain property. It simply means that if you choose to keep assets separate and apart, you had best inform your spouse as to what they are. Failure to abide by this basic principle is often fatal to the validity of the agreement and will cause it to be annulled in the future.

In addition, a prenuptial or postnuptial agreement will not enable you to terminate your spouse's rightful share unfairly or inappropriately. Most courts are quick to determine that if one of the spouses has been treated improperly or unfairly, the agreement will be set aside and the law of the state will prevail.

Additionally, trying to specify alimony or property settlement payments by using an agreement may be difficult to enforce because society as a rule tries to preserve marriage rather than facilitate divorce. There are exceptions. For example, New York state has provided by statute that prenuptial agreements may provide for the amount and duration of the support of a spouse and the custody, education, and support of a child or children under certain circumstances.

If your purpose in having a prenuptial agreement prepared is to avoid sharing assets with your future or present spouse or to hide these assets from the spouse, a prenuptial agreement is *not* for you. And perhaps marriage isn't either.

Regardless of the purpose of an individual agreement, it provides the contracting parties with a means of distributing assets at the conclusion of the marriage. The parties are creating a personal contract.

LOOK BEFORE YOU LEAP: IMPORTANT ISSUES

CHAPTER **4**
Conflicts of Law

The founding fathers never pictured commercial air travel or large national employers moving employees all over the nation. Neither was there any idea that we would be able to extend life to the point where retirement and leisure time would place large segments of society south in retirement areas of the "sun belt." Many people actually live in more than one place and consider their home to be in the state that taxes them the least.

To meet some of these complexities, an organization that has helped to make certain state laws uniform has adopted the Uniform Premarital Agreement Act. A copy of this law is in the appendix. Within the next several years it is expected that most states will adopt this law and help to make somewhat uniform the law regarding prenuptial agreements.

Which Law Applies

If a couple, both widowed, marry in Ohio and have a prenuptial agreement signed in Ohio before they marry, and then immediately move to Arizona where they had already found the house they intend to live out the rest of their years together in, and they begin a divorce in Arizona, which law applies? Is it the law of Ohio where the prenuptial agreement was prepared and signed, or Arizona, which is the state of the marital domicile? Lawyers call this general problem "conflicts of law." What is the law that applies?

The United States Constitution directs that each state "give full faith and credit" to the laws of each other state. Yet, when it comes to premarital agreements it is likely that the agreement will be judged by the law of the state in which it is tested, the state where the married couple lives. Even though every careful lawyer, when preparing a premarital agreement, will specify that it is to be interpreted under the laws of state "X," judges tend to apply concepts of fairness that are known to them; and a judge in state "Y" is likely to apply the law of state "Y" in interpreting the agreement.

How to Avoid Conflicts of Law

If you know before the marriage that you are likely to live in a different state after the marriage, you should either use a lawyer in the state you are going to live in, or have your lawyer consult with a lawyer in the state you are going to live in when the prenuptial agreement is prepared.

> Paula, recently divorced, went to her high school ten-year reunion and discovered that Bill, too, was just divorced. Paula was the heir to a large family fortune from her grandfather. Bill was the owner of a chain of successful stores in the Denver area. They intended to marry in Paula's home state of Illinois and then live in a suburb of Denver, where Paula had already selected a house.
>
> Paula consulted with her divorce lawyer in Illinois "to avoid making the same mistake twice." However, during the process of negotiations, Colorado law was thoroughly researched and a Colorado lawyer was engaged to review the ultimate agreement. The agreement was signed minutes before the wedding ceremony, but Paula and Bill had ample time to review it with their respective lawyers several weeks before the wedding.

It is imperative, if you know that you are going to be making your marital home in a certain state, that the law of that state and even a lawyer from that state be consulted before the agreement is signed and you marry. Once you have married, the agreement cannot be changed.

Summary

The laws of the state, not the federal government, apply to premarital agreements. Unfortunately the laws of each state are different, although efforts at uniformity are underway. If you know that after marriage you will be living in a different state, your lawyer should consult with a lawyer in that state, or you should get a lawyer in that state in the first place.

CHAPTER 5
Interfaith Marriage

There was a time when the emigration of groups to America resulted in ethnic neighborhoods, where "boy meets girl" was between the same religious and ethnic groups. As neighborhoods became older and decayed, and the migration to the suburbs from the cities resulted, the traditional ethnic lines fell. Along with the migration came substantial changes in the relationship many people had with their religion and church. College attendance became a usual experience for millions and the social revolution of the 1960s, coupled with the civil rights revolution, caused a mass change in the frequency of interfaith marriage. Although there was once a time when it was difficult to find a clergyman who would perform an interfaith marriage, the hunt for such clergy is rather easy today. Interfaith marriage is a part of American life and the American experience.

Bert and Ann met during their residency training as ophthalmic surgeons. He was raised a Jew and she, a Latter-day Saint. They married without the blessings of either of their families. After ten years of marriage they had a thriving surgery practice and four children. While flying back from a medical meeting in their own plane from Jackson Hole, Wyoming, there was a tragic accident and they and two of their four children died in the crash. The funeral was the first time their respective families were ever in the same room with each other, but not the last, because they battled over the custody of the two surviving boys.

Fortunately for the courts, Bert and Ann had wills, which both designated Ann's sister as the custodian of the children if they died. This enabled the courts to ignore the religious issues, at least head on, and place custody with the sister. She later adopted the children and raised them as Mormons.

Bert and Ann didn't have a prenuptial agreement. Most couples starting out in life don't. They never really came to terms with the religious differences of their background. The children celebrated both Christmas and Hanukkah. It was a home of no religion to speak of. Their wills did not deal explicitly with their wishes regarding religion for surviviors, but by their designating Ann's sister, a Mormon, as custodian, the courts were able to infer their intention.

In the past few years numerous cases of parental kidnapping, the abduction of a child by his or her own parent, have been reported in the news media. Many have involved marriage between American women and Middle Eastern men who are Muslim. Under Islamic law, children are the property of their father. Many of these men, faced during divorce proceedings with the prospects of losing their children, have taken them and returned to their homeland, and the mother of the children is faced with a complicated international custody case.

Couples, particularly young ones, believe they can overcome all obstacles to their marriage. Yet religion and tradition can become perplexing when children are born and their families are seeking them to follow the teachings and traditions of their respective backgrounds. Some resolution of these likely conflicts should be made before the marriage. When there is agreement, that agreement should be spelled out in their wills and a prenuptial agreement. Even if their marriage is wonderful, there is always the horrible possibility that they will die in a common disaster and their families will fight a battle over the children's custody that may have religious and ethnic overtones.

Indeed, other potential conflicts can be resolved in this way also. For instance, if one person is going to take time out from a career or education to further the career of the other, a premarital agreement can be very helpful in the event a divorce occurs before the spouse who gave up school can go back. Many misunderstandings about the very role each person will have in child rearing and homemaking can be worked out before the marriage, using the premarital agreement as the focal point for the finding of common understandings.

Summary

Although it is often believed that "love conquers all," there are religious and ethnic considerations that can best be worked out before children come along. These problems need not occur only if the marriage ends in divorce, but also if the couple are killed in a common disaster. Even the very role each person will have regarding responsibilities and roles in the marriage might better be worked out before the marriage than after.

CHAPTER 6

Children from Prior Marriages

One third of all people now getting married have been married before. Twenty percent of all marriages are between couples who have both been married before. By the time the children reach the seventh grade in school, one half of all children are no longer living with their mother and father. In fact, 20 percent of all children born in America are not born to a married couple at all. The subject of premarriage considerations would be incomplete without considering children from prior marriages.

Child Support

As a result of strong pressures by the federal government, virtually every state legislature has in the past two years adopted minimum guidelines for child support. These state laws affect your husband-to-be if he has children. If he is paying less than the minimum amount of support, he may be taken back to court to have his support raised.

Most states have provided that child support minimums are:

For one child	20 percent of net income
For two children	25 percent of net income
For three children	32 percent of net income

Therefore, you cannot plan on your fiancé always paying what he is now paying for support, particularly if he pays less than the prescribed minimum established in the state where his children live.

Many second marriages are viewed by the first spouse with jealousy and envy. Many couples return from a honeymoon to find legal documents waiting in the mailbox to increase child support. Therefore, you should never assume that your spouse's child support obligation will not change; it likely will change.

The Second Spouse's Income

Led by a California statute passed a few years ago, state after state, either by statute or case law and judicial interpretation, has begun to take into consideration the income of a second spouse. In 1988, both Illinois and Florida, for the first time, have recognized the reality of the entire family budget in judging the ability of a parent to pay increased child support.

Also, every state considers a divorced parent's obligation to his or her first family as of paramount importance to a new family of a second marriage. It is surprising how many people marry without having any idea that the person they marry has a severe arrearage in child support and is on the brink of being jailed for contempt of court. Often, a new spouse's entire assets are used just to resolve a child support arrearage and keep the new husband from going to jail for nonsupport. Be aware of the primary obligations that the law places on the duty to pay child support.

Alice came in with Don, clutching in her fist some papers. Upon review it seemed that Don had a child support arrearage of $2400 and was paying, when he paid at all, only 14 percent of his net earnings for support of his two teenage girls from his first marriage. This, under state law, had to be raised to a minimum of 25 percent of his net earnings. When the judge learned of the honeymoon cruise that Don and Alice had just returned from, he was likely to hold Don in contempt of court and jail him. Alice rendered the classic line, "Does the judge realize we have to live, too?"

In most states, the law will assume Alice knew all about Don's child support obligation and predicament before she married him. Yet, in truth, many women never ask about these issues and few husbands volunteer their financial plight. The first obligation of a parent is to the children of the first marriage.

Joint Custody

Most states during the 1960s adopted some form of joint custody. Some state laws permit it, some prefer it, and others require it. Whatever form it takes, these joint custody statutes attempt to treat life in a more realistic way: divorce severs the marriage, but not the relationship between a man and a woman as parents of children. Increasingly, children spend more time in the residences of both their parents. More than ever, it is likely that at some time during their period of minority, children may request a change in the principal residence.

Marrying someone who has children places you in a complex legal and social relationship as a stepparent. Often there is poor communication between former spouses and it takes the new spouse to serve as the go-between. You can expect that you will be called upon in many ways, both financially and personally, by the time the children finish college.

Summary

Marrying someone with children means you should be aware of the child support obligations and the fact that it will likely change in the future. Your income will be considered as well as the minimum guidelines that have been established. Joint custody will further involve everyone in the relationship with the children, both financially and in many other ways.

CHAPTER 7
Taxes

Tax Planning

There is some tax planning that should be considered when getting married. In order to file a personal tax return as a married person you must be married on December 31 of the tax year. Being married for the majority of the year doesn't count. One day is good enough: the last day of the year.

For the recipient of child support, alimony, or maintenance, there are tax implications to getting married for the second time. If quarterly estimates of income taxes have not been paid in, a tax deficiency can be avoided by a remarriage before the end of the year.

The Marriage Penalty

A few years ago, the tax rates for married people and single people became skewed in favor of single people and some couples got divorced to lower their income taxes. Congress, to rectify this, has enacted rules that help lower the tax rate for a spouse's income. Now it generally is the case that married people who file a joint return pay a lower tax than the same two taxpayers would pay if they were single and filing as separate taxpayers. The marriage penalty has been eliminated.

Taxpayer Responsibility

A word of caution: each taxpayer who signs a joint return is responsible for all of the information on the return and all of the taxes that are due or which the IRS may later determine are due. If you marry in December and file a joint tax return with your new spouse, you will be responsible for all the taxes owed.

There is an exception to this: If you are totally innocent of failing to report income that your spouse earned you may fall under the "innocent spouse rule" that Congress broadly expanded in the Divorce Reform Act, which became effective in 1985. If you can show that you had no knowledge of the income that wasn't reported you may be able to avoid the taxes and penalties.

The Prenuptial Agreement and Taxes

Remember that in a prenuptial agreement you can often change the way the law will deal with your assets and income if the marriage ends in divorce or death. Thus, you can provide that your spouse must pay all of the taxes and protect you from a claim by the IRS of a tax deficiency and penalties.

Leo never told Dawn that he was skimming income at the restaurant and they filed joint income tax returns for the three years they were married. Knowing the nature of Leo's business, Dawn's lawyer negotiated for a clause in the prenuptial agreement to "hold Dawn harmless" from any taxes or penalties. Thus, whether Dawn falls under the innocent spouse rule or not, she is protected by the prenuptial agreement.

There are many other tax considerations. For example, if one spouse has a great deal of income that is from tax free municipal bonds, they may find after marriage that there are income taxes to be paid that haven't been planned for.

Federal estate tax consequences should be considered when entering into a prenuptial agreement. It should be noted that the first $600,000 of an estate is exempt from all federal estate taxes. Above that amount, there are certain advantages to leaving up to 50 percent of the estate to the surviving spouse—including paying less to the federal government and more to your relatives. This desirable avenue should be taken through your will, not the prenuptial agreement. However, some states have provided that anything left to a spouse through a prenuptial agreement is deemed to be the payment of a contractual debt and, therefore, not subject to state inheritance taxation. Each state must be dealt with individually and your attorney should be consulted concerning the specifics.

Tax Return Exchange

Your lawyer and accountant should review your prospective spouse's last several years of tax returns. Not only will this permit better tax planning for you, but the tax returns are one of the best indicators of the assets and income and sources of income of your prospective spouse. An unwillingness to permit your advisers to examine these important documents may indicate that there is some secret your new spouse doesn't want you to know. It also may tell you that the person you are planning to marry is not willing to be totally open with you. A tendency to be secretive before marriage does not bode well for a free and open marriage.

Summary

To file as a joint married taxpayer you must be married on the last day of the year only. When you sign a joint tax return with your spouse you are fully responsible for the taxes owed, no matter whose income it really was. Tax returns from prior years are very helpful to your attorney.

CHAPTER **8**

Estate Planning

What Is an Estate Plan?

An estate plan is a direction of what is to be done with property, not only when someone dies, but also when someone is still living. The tools lawyers use for an estate plan are wills, trusts, gifts, joint tenancies, and insurance. The estate plan, or absence of an estate plan, vastly affects the entire way property is to be treated in a marriage.

Most people who contemplate a premarital agreement give little thought to the estate plan and many lawyers will prepare a premarital agreement without preparing the wills, trusts, and other documents that will help the premarital agreement or defeat its purpose.

Use of Wills

Many premarital agreements attempt to preserve for someone's children the assets they had before the second marriage. They want those assets to go to their children, not to their new spouse, if they die. Yet it is a will that controls how assets upon death will be treated. A premarital agreement is not a will. There is a special formalism to a will, and how it is signed and prepared, that makes it entirely different from a premarital agreement.

In most states you cannot completely disinherit your spouse or leave your widow or widower with nothing upon your death. However that entirely understandable goal can be obtained through the use of trusts, gifts, joint tenancy title, and insurance.

Before the premarital agreement is entered into, not only should you and your lawyer learn all you can about the assets of your new spouse, but also know all you can about the entire estate plan. Is title in joint tenancy with any other person? Is there a trust that controls the assets now or will control the assets at death? And what does the will currently say?

A will is only effective upon death. So whatever the will provides for can be changed and changed again. It only counts when death occurs. But the prenuptial agreement can dictate what the will must provide for you, and then if the will is changed you have a legal basis to complain.

Joint Tenancy Property

The most frequently used device for estate planning is the use of joint tenancy as the method to hold title to any asset. From title to a house, a car, and dozens of bank accounts, holding the asset in joint tenancy with another person is the single most popular estate planning tool in America.

There are many things about this popular method of holding title that are misunderstood. For example: Many people believe that property held in joint tenancy, such as a bank account, is really the property of the person whose name is listed first on the account. This is not true. In the eyes of the law, each person whose name is on the account is an owner. Joint tenancy property automatically passes to the surviving joint tenant if one joint tenant dies. It doesn't matter what the will says, and most important, it doesn't matter what the prenuptial agreement says.

Ralph and Sally got married, each for the second time. Ralph wanted his business and all his other assets to go to his children when he died, except for his home, which he agreed Sally would have. Years earlier Ralph had put the title to his house in joint tenancy with Bob, who never approved of his father's remarriage. Because the house was in joint tenancy, Bob ended up with it even though the prenuptial agreement provided otherwise. Sally got nothing.

This can be prevented by thoroughly understanding how title to all property is held. No matter what the good intentions of the prenuptial agreement, if property is held in joint tenancy and your spouse dies, it is the other joint tenant who will get the property.

Trusts

A trust is the transfer of property to a trustee, for the benefit of someone else, the beneficiary. There are two kinds of trusts: living trusts and trusts created by will. Whichever kind of trust, it will often defeat the purposes of a prenuptial agreement. Much like joint tenancy, the law will follow the trust provisions.

Trusts can also be used to make sure that you or your intended spouse get what you want them to get. Many children or other relatives do not approve of the intended spouse in a second marriage, and there can be a good deal of fighting, court battles, and money spent on lawyers after you die. A trust is an excellent way to avoid this and to augment your prenuptial agreement.

Gifts

One way to ensure that the person you want to get your property does, is to give it to him or her during your lifetime, and before the marriage.

No one disagreed with Bill's plan. He would marry Ann but he wanted his son, Bill, Jr., to get the bulk of his large estate. To button it all down he gave his son three fourths of his large estate before he married Ann. After ten years, Ann sued him for divorce and attacked the validity of the premarital agreement, which dealt with what would happen to property upon death, but never mentioned the demise of the marriage by divorce. But because of the large gift to Bill, Jr., the attack on the premarital contract, even if successful, would not put back into the marriage the large gift made to Bill, Jr., before the marriage.

A gift is the perfect estate plan tool. And just as it can be used in one way, so too, it can be used in another.

CHAPTER **9**

Planting the Idea in Your Fiancé's Mind

Ted, a successful surgeon, had been married 30 years. But, with children almost through college, the marriage did not withstand the empty nest test. He willingly parted with half of his $1 million in assets and liberal alimony to marry Myra, who had a net worth one twentieth of his and an income one tenth of his.

When asked to consider a prenuptial agreement, Dr. Ted had said, "Are you kidding? We are in love!"

The single greatest barrier to a prenuptial agreement for most people is the unwillingness to raise the subject with their fiancé. "I just couldn't mention such a thing!" is the usual excuse. The inability or unwillingness to discuss the subject is the usual reason no prenuptial agreement is ever negotiated before the marriage.

The reasons for this are:

1. Most people feel that talk about money and property is "not romantic" and will detract from the joy they feel about the impending marriage.

2. Most people feel that talk about money and property will communicate distrust and lack of commitment to the marriage.

3. Many people, particularly women, are not assertive and are highly trusting.

4. Many people have bad feelings about their divorces and their

prior dealings with the legal system and lawyers.

5. Some people don't do a very good job planning and organizing anything.

6. Some people don't want to spend money on lawyer's fees.

7. Most people think that a prenuptial agreement concerns only the marriage ending in divorce, and don't consider its value as a tool if the marriage ends in death. (Remember, all marriages end one way or the other.)

8. Some people are put off by the requirement in most states that there must be a full and complete disclosure of all assets and income.

9. Some people don't realize that a plan, which includes a prenuptial agreement and a will, can accomplish a great deal.

Getting It Started

It is never too soon to tell someone you are seeing that you consider a prenuptial agreement as something that you would want to consider if you ever married (or married again). The sooner you state your desire and intention, the more likely it is that you will be able to proceed in a logical way in planning the wedding and the property and tax aspects of marriage. The longer your intended spouse knows your position, the longer he or she has to get used to it and accept it. So the sooner you raise it the better.

One means of discussion, which appeals to many people, is to call a prenuptial agreement "an estate plan." For example: "John, I think we should consider a complete estate plan before we get married." Obviously by the term "complete estate plan" you mean a prenuptial agreement. But, you need not say this at first. Few people will become alarmed by this approach.

Being forthright, open, and honest is good not only when a relationship becomes serious enough to consider marriage, but being open and honest is the best way for the marriage to survive after you tie the knot. It is not a good idea to have a hidden agenda.

Robert K. felt that if he told Madelyn he wanted a prenuptial agreement, he might plant seeds of distrust. He also was afraid of losing her. So he spent countless hours with his lawyer learning the rules in his state for nonmarital property. His plan was a secret one. He would never put anything in Madelyn's name and would keep all his property separate from her. After a few years Madelyn felt that Robert wasn't fully sharing with her, which of course he wasn't. Her perception of distrust on his part made her feel that she did not have the security she thought she would have in the marriage. Their relationship became polarized because Robert felt that she was overly concerned with "his assets." These feelings by each of them ultimately led to a divorce.

There are countless marriages that end for just such a reason. A prenuptial agreement, instead of a hidden plan, avoids appearing selfish and secretive. Knowing clearly what's yours and what is your spouse's will aid the relationship and vastly increase the chance for the marriage to succeed.

The problems of Madelyn and Robert are reenacted in divorce courts all over this country every day. The mortality rate for second marriages is higher than for first marriages. In many places in the United States, the divorce rate for second marriages is 75 percent! Many of these divorces are the result of perceived selfishness by one spouse toward the other. Feelings of insecurity and distrust are one of the major causes of divorce among second marriages and people who marry for the first time after having an established career.

This can all be avoided by a frank and open discussion as to what you really intend to share and not share before the marriage. After all, if your intended spouse doesn't agree with your plan for the assets, isn't it best to know that before the marriage? A prenuptial or premarital agreement can go a long way toward allowing both parties to put their cards on the table.

Without question a prenuptial agreement is a difficult subject to raise. Many people begin the discussion by voicing their concern for their children from a prior marriage. Others begin by saying that they place great trust in their lawyers and follow their lawyers' advice. You might even get the subject out in the open by suggesting that your fiancé read this book so that together you can discuss the ideas and issues raised.

Few people will back out of an engagement to marry because of the terms of a prenuptial agreement. Most agreements are quite fair to both spouses, particularly where one spouse has a far larger estate than the other. Lawyers are cautious in preparing the agreement to make sure that it is legally enforceable. They strive for the fairness that they know will help the agreement withstand the tests that may occur in a court of law. The very process of discussing these matters, assets, and income, helps the relationship mature toward the good trusting relationship that every marriage must have to survive.

Summary

Although it is hard to raise the subject of a premarital agreement, the first time, one way is to begin by discussing "an estate plan." Many marriages are destroyed because a husband or wife is trying to keep his or her property separate. Feelings of distrust are inevitable. The process of openly discussing the matters necessary in a prenuptial agreement helps forge a trusting relationship between husband and wife.

THE EASY PART: PRACTICAL MATTERS

CHAPTER 10
Getting to Know Yourself

In order for you to be successful in your search for the best prenuptial agreement you must know what you are looking for.

It is well worth the time and effort to analyze the inner you—discover what you really desire. Socrates had a point when he said that the basis of wisdom is self-knowledge and from that an awareness of all other knowledge can be acquired. Surely it is impossible to understand everything until you understand yourself.

Self-Analysis Quiz

Following is a number of questions that will hopefully give you some insight into your preferences. A space is provided for your answer.

1. Who is your first consideration?

    (a) Intended spouse   _____
    (b) Children by a prior marriage   _____

2. Who would need your money the most?

    (a) Intended spouse   _____
    (b) Children by a prior marriage   _____

3. Can you set aside enough money or assets so that your children will be taken care of for life?

    (a) Yes   _____
    (b) No   _____

4. If you set aside money or other assets for your children, will anything be left for your intended spouse?

    (a) Yes   _____

    (b) No   _____

5. Can you acquire enough life insurance to take care of your children and/or your intended spouse?

    (a) Yes   _____

    (b) No   _____

6. Are there possessions you want your children to have now rather than upon your death?

    (a) Yes   _____

    (b) No   _____

An Analysis of Your Answers

1. If your answer was (a), let your attorney know. Keep it foremost in your mind when finalizing your decisions concerning the agreement.

    If your answer is (b), you should still notify your attorney.

2. If your answer is (a), steps can be taken to obviate the problem through your agreement. Consider leaving your intended spouse a life estate, giving the children money now, or buying additional life insurance. Obviously, you and your attorney should discuss this fully.

    If your answer is (b), then the opposite is true. Considerations should be made to provide for your children's needs. If you cannot answer this question, you're having problems. Think twice before entering into an agreement.

3. If your answer is (a), you are indeed blessed. You need only consider whether you have enough for yourself and your intended spouse for the rest of your lives.

    If your answer is (b), then you must carefully consider whom you wish to take care of financially. Reconsider questions 1 and 2.

4. If your answer is (a), then once again you and your intended spouse should have no problems with drawing up an agreement.

   If your answer is (b), then you should give due consideration to this obvious problem and refer to questions 1 and 2.

5. If your answer is (a), then you must ask yourself whether your children will be satisfied emotionally with life insurance policy money as opposed to individual stock, real estate, and so on. Emotional considerations are of primary importance when there is enough money to go around. Ask your children if they have any emotional, rather than monetary, interest in any of your assets.

   If your answer is (b), then maybe you should consider acquiring life insurance policies in order to take care of your intended spouse, who probably has no emotional attachment to particular assets.

6. If your answer is (a), then due consideration should be given to the possessions and the children. Consideration should be given to the depletion of your assets and its affect on your future. If your answer is (b), then please discontinue consideration of this question.

Personal Evaluation Work Sheet

	YES	NO	HAVE TO THINK ABOUT IT
Do you wish to avoid future problems?	—	—	—
Have you had problems in your prior marriage(s)?	—	—	—
Has your intended spouse had problems in his/her prior marriage(s)?	—	—	—
Is it necessary to provide for your children now?	—	—	—

	YES	NO	HAVE TO THINK ABOUT IT
Is it necessary to provide for your children later?	—	—	—
Do you wish to provide for your children now?	—	—	—
Do you wish to provide for your children later?	—	—	—
Do you wish to provide for your intended spouse's children now?	—	—	—
Do you wish to provide for your intended spouse's children later?	—	—	—
Are you really in love?	—	—	—

Have you discussed and anticipated such problems as:

Religion	—	—	—
Sex	—	—	—
Time devoted to your work	—	—	—
Time devoted to your spouse's work	—	—	—
Division of income between different categories of expenditures	—	—	—
Signing this agreement	—	—	—
Do you really wish to have this agreement?	—	—	—

	YES	NO	HAVE TO THINK ABOUT IT
Does your intended spouse really wish to have this agreement?	—	—	—

Now review all of your answers. Remember, this is not a test There are no right or wrong answers. The only intent is to make you think.

CHAPTER 11

Gathering the Facts

This chapter will provide you with a list of documents needed for preparing a prenuptial agreement. Take this list with you when you see your attorney for the first time.

This list is not meant to be all-inclusive, but it is meant to be a guide.

Necessary Documents

In order to be as sure as possible that a court will not declare the prenuptial agreement to be fraudulent, it is important that any list of assets and debts be complete. It is absolutely essential that you gather all documents that you possibly can concerning assets, income, and liabilities. It should be noted that the following list is not exhaustive because there always are some assets or debts that may be out of the ordinary. Add your own items.

1. Individual tax returns for the past five years—the purpose of this is not only to give your potential spouse full knowledge of your income, but also make you aware of assets often listed on tax returns.

2. All bank savings account statements (for four to five years, if possible).

3. All checking account statements (as well as all checks for the past five years). By reviewing your cancelled checks, you will be able to recall major assets or purchases you made.

4. All money market statements (for five years if possible, as well as all cancelled checks from these accounts).

5. All W-2 forms.

6. A copy of all pension plans.

7. A copy of all pension plan statements for the past five years.

8. A copy of all profit-sharing plans.

9. A copy of all profit-sharing plan statements.

10. A copy of all Keogh statements for the past five years.

11. A copy of all 401-K statements for the past five years.

12. A list and copy of IRA statements for the past five years.

13. A copy of all health insurance plans and statements for the past three years.

14. A copy of all life insurance policies and plans.

15. A copy of all annuity purchases.

16. A list and copy of all credit card agreements on which you have personal liability.

17. A copy of all credit agreements on which you have personal liability.

18. A copy of all financial statements submitted by you to any entity or institution over the past five years.

19. A list of all safety deposit boxes.

20. A list of the contents of all safety deposit boxes.

21. A list of all debts.

22. A list of all other types of liabilities.

23. A list of all bonds (including value at the present time, purchase cost, and how acquired).

24. A list of all stock held by you (including purchase price, number of shares, present value, and how acquired).

25. A copy of all stock certificates held by you.

26. A copy of all records concerning the purchase of the previously mentioned stocks and bonds.

27. The name of every person having a joint or co-interest with you concerning these bonds.

28. The name of every person having a joint or co-interest with you concerning these stocks.

29. An inventory of all antiques (including date and cost of acquisition, your best estimate of their fair market value, the name and address of each person or entity having a security interest and nature of this interest, and the balance due on this obligation and extent of the default should there be one).

30. An inventory of all paintings (including date and cost of acquisition, your best estimate of their fair market value, the name and address of each person or entity having a security interest and nature of this interest, and the balance due on this obligation and extent of the default should there be one).

31. An inventory of all artworks (including date and cost of acquisition, your best estimate of their fair market value, the name and address of each person or entity having a security interest and the nature of this interest, and the balance due on this obligation and extent of the default should there be one).

32. An inventory of all jewelry (including date and cost of acquisition, your best estimate of their fair market value, the name

and address of each person or entity having a security interest and nature of this interest, and the balance due on this obligation and extent of the default should there be one).

33. An inventory of all other personal property (including date and cost of acquisition, your best estimate of their fair market value, the name and address of each person or entity having a security interest and nature of this interest, and the balance due on this obligation and extent of the default should there be one).

34. A list of all partnerships in which you have an interest.

35. A copy of any and all partnership returns concerning the partnerships you have listed above.

36. A list of all limited partnerships in which you are involved (along with all tax returns concerning these limited partnerships and K-1 forms concerning these partnerships).

37. A list of all interest in businesses that you may have in which you have proprietary interests (such as joint ventures)(for each such interest for proprietorships, partnerships, or corporations, set forth the value of the interests, the type of interests that you have in the business, purchase price, the present value, and how you acquired same).

38. Prior divorce judgment(s) (including all settlement agreements that were or were not made a part of the divorce judgment as well as any postjudgment determinations as to monies due and owing, and any support obligations for prior wives or husbands or children of a prior marriage.

39. A list of all real estate that you own (including date purchased, purchase price, present assessment, and estimated present value).

40. A list of mortgages (including a list of judgments on the property, list of second mortgages on the property as well as any other mortgages, a list of any other liens including tax

liens. If any of this property is jointly owned, the nature of this ownership).

41. All employment contracts for the past five years.

42. A list of all leaseholds (including copies of leases, dates or termination of lease, estimated value, and how acquired).

43. A list of all interest in money, real estate, or other assets, which you may have in the form of residuary life estate from another person (all information concerning this should be attendant to this list and include relevant documents including estimated evaluations).

44. A list of all entities in which you're acting as a fiduciary concerning any and all assets.

45. A list of all suits in which you are involved or are anticipating to be involved.

46. A list of all collections you may have (including stamps, coins, baseball cards, comic books, movies, autographs, books, and photographs).

47. A list of all monies and/or accounts for items that are due and owing to you either now or in the future.

48. A list of all trusts of which you may be a beneficiary now or in the future.

49. A list of all prospects of inheritance from any person whether living or dead or whether the interest is vested or nonvested.

50. Anything and everything else that you can possibly think of.

Self-Interview Worksheets

The self-interview worksheet will help you prepare a document for your initial interview with your attorney. This will save the attorney time and save you money in the form of attorney's fees.

NAME: _____

STREET ADDRESS(ES): _____

CITY: _____

STATE: _____

ZIP CODE: _____

HOME TELEPHONE: _____

BUSINESS TELEPHONE: _____

YOUR SOCIAL SECURITY NUMBER: _____

AGE (BIRTHDATE): _____

NAME OF INTENDED SPOUSE: _____

PRESENT STREET ADDRESS(ES): _____

CITY: _____

STATE: _____

ZIP CODE: _____

HOME TELEPHONE OF INTENDED SPOUSE: _____

BUSINESS TELEPHONE OF INTENDED SPOUSE: _____

AGE (BIRTHDATE) OF INTENDED SPOUSE: _____

SOCIAL SECURITY NUMBER OF INTENDED SPOUSE: _____

NAME OF ATTORNEY OF INTENDED SPOUSE: _____

ADDRESS OF ATTORNEY OF INTENDED SPOUSE: _____

TELEPHONE NUMBER OF ATTORNEY OF INTENDED SPOUSE:

_____

NUMBER OF PRIOR MARRIAGE(S): _____

NAMES OF CHILDREN OF PRIOR MARRIAGE(S)

(INCLUDING BIRTHDATES):

_____

_____

_____

_____

EDUCATIONAL BACKGROUND:

    HIGH SCHOOL _____

    COLLEGE DEGREE(S) _____

    ADVANCED DEGREE(S) _____

    OTHER _____

MILITARY SERVICE: _____

INTENDED SPOUSE'S NAME: _____

PRIOR MARRIAGE(S) OF INTENDED SPOUSE: _____

NAMES AND AGES OF CHILDREN OF PRIOR MARRIAGE(S) OF

    INTENDED SPOUSE:

    _____

    _____

    _____

    _____

    _____

EDUCATIONAL BACKGROUND OF INTENDED SPOUSE:

    HIGH SCHOOL _____

    COLLEGE DEGREE(S) _____

    ADVANCED DEGREE(S) _____

    OTHER _____

MILITARY SERVICE OF INTENDED SPOUSE: _____

ASSETS:

    REAL ESTATE AND OTHER REAL PROPERTY _____

    BANK ACCOUNTS _____

    CERTIFICATES OF DEPOSIT _____

    OTHER LIQUID MONIES _____

    VEHICLES _____

    PERSONAL PROPERTY _____

    STOCKS _____

BONDS _____

PENSIONS _____

PROFIT SHARING _____

RETIREMENT PLANS _____

IRAs _____

401-Ks _____

CLOSED CORPORATIONS _____

BUSINESSES _____

PARTNERSHIPS _____

LIFE INSURANCE POLICIES _____

ANNUITIES _____

KEOGH PLANS _____

FURNITURE _____

COLLECTIONS _____

MORTGAGES _____

EMPLOYMENT CONTRACTS _____

INHERITANCES AND TRUSTS _____

OTHER _____

LIABILITIES:

    MORTGAGES ON REAL ESTATE INCLUDING NAMES OF

     ALL RESPONSIBLE PARTIES _____

    SHORT-TERM DEBT _____

    LONG-TERM DEBT _____

    REVOLVING CHARGES _____

    CONTINGENT LIABILITY _____

MONTHLY EXPENSES (THIS CAN BE DONE AS WEEKLY OR YEARLY)

    RENTAL EXPENSE _____

    HEAT _____

    ELECTRIC _____

GAS _____

INSURANCE _____

PARKING _____

MAINTENANCE _____

OTHER _____

MORTGAGE(S) _____

REAL ESTATE TAXES _____

HOME OWNER'S INSURANCE _____

REPAIRS _____

MAINTENANCE _____

HEAT _____

ELECTRIC _____

GAS _____

WATER _____

SEWER _____

REMOVAL OF GARBAGE _____

OTHER _____

TELEPHONE _____

PLUMBING EXPENSES _____

ELECTRICAL EXPENSES _____

EQUIPMENT AND FURNISHINGS _____

AUTO PAYMENT _____

AUTO INSURANCE COSTS _____

REGISTRATION FOR AUTO _____

LICENSING COSTS _____

MAINTENANCE COSTS _____

FUEL AND OIL COSTS _____

COMMUTING COSTS _____

REPAIR COSTS _____

OTHER _____

FOOD _____

CLOTHING _____

MEDICAL PRESCRIPTION DRUGS _____

NONMEDICAL PRESCRIPTION DRUGS _____

RESTAURANTS _____

CLOTHING _____

DRY CLEANING _____

DOMESTIC HELP _____

MEDICAL EXPENSES _____

PSYCHIATRIC EXPENSES _____

DENTAL EXPENSES _____

MEMBERSHIPS _____

CLUB DUES _____

SPORTS _____

HOBBIES _____

VACATIONS _____

SCHOOL COSTS _____

ENTERTAINMENT _____

TOBACCO AND ALCOHOL _____

NEWSPAPERS _____

PERIODICALS _____

GIFTS _____

CONTRIBUTIONS _____

ALIMONY FOR PRIOR MARRIAGE(S) _____

CHILD SUPPORT FOR PRIOR MARRIAGE(S) _____

LIFE INSURANCE COSTS _____

INDIVIDUAL CREDIT CARD COSTS _____

OTHER _____

After you have read this book, made your decision to have an agreement drawn up, completed the preceding worksheets, and collected all documents, you are ready to see your attorney.

CHAPTER **12**

How to Choose a Lawyer

Must You Choose a Lawyer?

There is no legal requirement that you need a lawyer to prepare a prenuptial agreement for you. This is no different from most legal matters: You can go into court to represent yourself, as well as prepare your own deeds, will, and any other legal documents you can manage. Forms and examples of prenuptial agreements are in the appendix.

Yet, there is an old adage among lawyers: A lawyer who represents himself in court has "a fool for a client." The few hundred dollars you save in legal fees could and likely will come to haunt you or your relatives in the future.

Do Lawyers Specialize?

We have all become accustomed to the current specialization of medicine divided according to the various systems and organs of the body. There are eye doctors, heart specialists, and experts in the digestive system.

Lawyers likewise are quite specialized. As a result of a 1974 United States Supreme Court decision, lawyers can advertise. The Supreme Court reasoned that advertising would help the public identify competent lawyers and make legal fees competitive. A typical yellow pages ad looks something like this:

Law offices of Cheatem and Howe, practice in the fields of admiralty, zoning, divorce, personal injury, workers compensation, corporations, and anything else you need or we can think up.

The ability of lawyers to be certified specialists is regulated by the bar associations of each state, and vary quite widely. Arizona (where the first advertising was permitted), California, and Florida have certified specialization, along with many other states. Several states permit lawyers, without any requirement whatsoever, to state that their practice is "concentrated" in a particular field. The traditional division in England between barristers (trial lawyers) and solicitors (office lawyers) never made it across the Atlantic during the colonial period. Yet that traditional dichotomy, between lawyers who go to court and lawyers who generally don't, exists in the United States. It is less formal, and with a bit of investigating on your part you can find a lawyer competent and versed in your needs.

Lists and Recommendations

There are more than 900,000 lawyers in the United States. In fact, there are more than 100,000 in California alone. Most of them are bright, intelligent, and well versed in some particular field of law or another.

More prenuptial agreements have been held invalid and unenforceable because of lawyer error than because of client error. Selecting the right lawyer for you is exceedingly important.

The fields of law that would give a lawyer the training and experience to prepare what you need are divorce (sometimes called "family law"), estate planning, and contract drafting. A healthy helping of negotiation skill is also very useful. Many lawyers possess these skills, practicing in large and small firms, huge cities, suburbs, and small towns. The best way to find the right lawyer for you is to research the matter.

Martindale and Hubbel is a seven-volume directory listing almost every lawyer in the United States. The listing is by state, and then by city. Each lawyer's essential biographical information is listed: Date of birth, date admitted to practice, and schools attended. Most important of all, each lawyer has one of four ratings: A, B, C, or unrated. The ratings are based on surveys made secretly by the staff of Martindale among lawyers and judges. There is also a paid advertisement section in which lawyers list their representative clients and fields of law practice. *Martindale and Hubbel* is available in most public libraries and the law library in the local county courthouse, which is open to the public.

There are several specialized legal organizations to which lawyers who regularly prepare prenuptial agreements belong. The American Academy of Matrimonial Lawyers is a national fellowship of lawyers who are noted experts in family law matters and generally held in high regard by fellow lawyers. They have passed stringent board exams and exceed at least seven years in specialization. Chapters are located in most of the populated states. You can find fellows in your area by contacting:

American Academy of Matrimonial Lawyers
20 North Michigan Avenue
Chicago, Illinois 60602
(312) 263-6477

The American Bar Association (ABA) numbers over 150,000 lawyers. Most of them are members of a smaller, special interest section of the association. The sections of family law and estate planning have members throughout the country who most likely are able to help you. For a list of members of the family law section and the estate planning section contact:

American Bar Association
750 North Lake Shore Drive
Chicago, Illinois 60611
(312) 988-5000

Likewise, state and large city bar associations can provide you with lists of lawyers who are members of special interest groups in these same fields of law. Be aware, however, that generally a revolving referral system has been established and the name you are given may be the next lawyer who is due to receive a referral in the registry. That lawyer may or may not be competent to handle your task.

Personal Recommendations

"Mr. Jones, you may not remember me; you represented me when I purchased my house on Maple Street several years ago. I thought you were quite competent in the handling of that matter and I wonder if you can recommend someone who is quite well versed in

DON'T GET MARRIED UNTIL YOU READ THIS

preparing nuptial agreements, someone who does them regularly." Mr. Jones may claim to be just the lawyer for you once again, but, if you press a bit, most lawyers will identify someone in their firm or in the community who might be right for you.

Conflicts of Interest

One of the requirements for a valid prenuptial agreement is that each prospective spouse reveal all of his or her income and assets. To do this effectively you should go to your own lawyer and not your fiancé's lawyer. Many states require that there be independent legal counsel for each person in order for the agreement to be viewed as fair.

> Marilyn M. came to see me and told me that, strange as it might seem, she had fallen in love with a man who is 27 years her senior and a friend of her father. He had been widowed for many years and insisted on a prenuptial agreement and that his trusted corporate lawyer must prepare it.
> A review of the proposed agreement revealed that Marilyn would live well on a beautiful 18-acre wooded estate in a grand mansion with servants, but when old Homer died she would be out in the cold and a bird society would receive everything. Marilyn was a nurse. When I pointed out to her and Homer's lawyer that he was getting a full-time nurse for life and she was giving up job security, we were able to negotiate a prenuptial contract in which she received $100,000 for each year they were married and would be permitted to stay in the mansion for five years after his death. If the marriage ended in divorce, she would receive $500,000 plus $100,000 for each year of marriage.

In that negotiation I pointed out to Homer's corporate lawyer that if Homer wasn't more generous, I would render a written legal opinion that the bargain Homer was offering was "non-negotiable." As an experienced lawyer in preparing prenuptial agreements, it was my legal opinion that his agreement was legally unenforceable. Yes, Marilyn would have signed it, but she would have tucked my letter away and probably used it years later. They wisely decided that negotiating a fair agreement with two lawyers was better than taking the risk of using one and ending up with an unenforceable prenuptial agreement.

Summary

Using a lawyer is probably wiser than not. There are many available listings of lawyers who are likely to be proficient in preparing prenuptial agreements. Don't go to a lawyer who is closely tied with your prospective spouse. Go to someone new and independent.

CHAPTER **13**
Legal Fees

Once you find an attorney whom you believe to have the proper and appropriate qualifications, you need to discuss fees. Fees for drafting an agreement can vary greatly from attorney to attorney and from law firm to law firm. They may very well depend on a number of different factors, including proximity to a large metropolitan area, size of the law firm, experience and reputation of the attorney, and complexity of the document. Other factors are the length of time the attorney must spend assimilating the information and preparing the papers. You must completely understand the basis for the fee that you are going to be charged. By the end of your initial discussion you should have a written fee agreement before you allow work to begin. A sample agreement is located in the appendix of this book.

Lawyers generally charge their clients on one of three bases—an hourly fee, a flat fee, or a contingency fee. A contingency fee is a percentage fee based on the recovery by a client as a result, generally, of a litigated matter and is irrelevant here.

Hourly Fee

You will most likely be charged on an hourly fee basis. It will be directly related to the time an attorney spends on every aspect of your case. Every lawyer within a firm generally has an hourly rate that he or she charges. It is based on reputation, specialty, size of the law firm, and the going rates of attorneys' fees in the area.

An attorney who is connected to a large city law firm is likely to charge more than a solo practitioner in a small town. Within a single large law firm, hourly rates may vary as much as $100 or more per hour. Partners generally charge more than their associates because the partner has the experience and reputation that draw clients to the firm in the first place.

When you are charged an hourly rate, you are charged for the actual time that a lawyer has spent on your agreement. These charges include all of your meetings as well as all of your phone calls. They include the research, the rough draft, review, revision, and final review of the document.

Most attorneys record their time in hourly segments. Depending on the law firm, billing is based on the quarter of an hour or tenth of an hour. The difference between these charges can be quite significant; for instance, if a lawyer has a billing rate of $100 per hour and the charge is based on the quarter hour, you generally will be charged $25 for 15 minutes or less. If you call your attorney to learn of the progress of your agreement and talk for five minutes, you generally will be charged the full $25. If, on the other hand, your lawyer bills based on tenths of an hour, he or she records his time on six minute intervals. In this type of scenario, each tenth of an hour costs $10. If you make the same five minute telephone call to this attorney, you will be charged for one tenth of an hour, or $10.

Make sure that you know exactly how you will be charged when you hire your attorney. If it is your attorney's policy to bill on a quarter hour basis, you may want to negotiate for smaller increments.

Flat Fee

Some attorneys charge a flat fee. This is rather unlikely because every document is usually drafted from scratch and takes considerable time. However, some attorneys draft prenuptial agreements on a very routine basis by using predrafted forms. If this is acceptable to you, make sure you understand exactly what the fee includes. Many times charges will be added, should the agreement take more time than anticipated or if there are last minute changes.

Be very, very wary of any attorney who gives you a flat fee for prenuptial agreements before you explain all of the particulars of your situation. An attorney who is quick to quote a flat fee before hearing about any customized research or drafting is probably not the best choice.

Costs Are Additional

Almost every lawyer's bill is broken down into at least two charges—costs and fees. The lawyer's fee has already been described. Costs are additional and are something to consider when estimating the total price of your agreement. The way a lawyer bills for costs will vary, but usually includes long distance telephone calls, photocopying, postage, and travel expenses. Check with your lawyer to find out how much you will be billed for them. They can be significant and it is your responsibility to understand all aspects.

Keeping Your Costs Down

Regardless of whether you decide to use a small town lawyer or a senior partner, you can save costs. After you discuss price with your attorney and decide to retain him or her, have a work session to decide the content of your agreement. Come to this meeting well prepared.

Take some sample clauses to your attorney's office to show him or her what you believe you need. This will enable him to understand your wishes more quickly. Also take a list of all of your assets and supporting documentation. Doing this will probably save you hundreds of dollars from the start.

Second, try to make all of your alterations in a single meeting. Remember, every time you change your mind or alter an agreement, the attorney is spending extra time, which means extra money. This doesn't mean you can't change your mind on an issue that is important. You must be happy with the agreement in its final form.

Third, if you must call your attorney, outline in advance all of the things you wish to discuss. Write down every question and have a pen and pad ready. Don't waste time making small talk.

Finally, make sure your agreement is not too cumbersome. You want to protect your assets and your future. Make sure that you and your partner understand the purpose of the agreement. You are not trying to chart a course for your entire life. You are only preventing problems from complicating it.

Take your time. Being prepared will save you money.

CHAPTER **14**
Being a Good Client

Arrive on Time

After you have chosen an attorney and agreed upon a manner of billing that is mutually satisfactory, you are ready to begin work. Always arrive on time for your appointment. If you arrive early, you may have to wait. Your attorney may be with another client or may be out of the office on another matter. But don't keep your attorney waiting. The time may very well be charged to you if your attorney is reading your file. Call ahead if you know you are going to be late or have to reschedule.

Dress Properly

There is no need to purchase a suit if you don't normally wear one. By the same token, you are meeting in a professional atmosphere and your mode of dress sends out signals to others. Dress in a manner that shows you are well informed, confident of your intentions, and serious about achieving results.

Be Prepared

Always arrive ready to work. Don't schedule an appointment until you have done your homework. You have already decided what the purpose of the agreement is, what it must include, and what you and your partner are willing to give up in order to achieve your mutual goals. Be prepared to be able to make full financial disclosure and answer any personal questions. To do otherwise would be a waste of time and money. Being prepared will establish your credibility and foster mutual respect.

Analyzing your desires will enable you to prepare the appropriate documentation. The documents listed in Chapter XI will guide you in thinking about which assets you're specifically looking to protect and those you may be willing to relinquish.

Bring the financial information to your attorney's office for your first meeting, specifically, your most recent tax returns. Bring a list of all your real property, all stocks and bonds that do not appear on your return, and all your cash. Be sure that your list of financial assets as well as debts is complete.

Be Honest

Your attorney is bound to keep your information confidential unless you give him or her the authority to release it. Illegally obtained assets must be listed so that your attorney may evaluate their importance. Be prepared to answer any personal questions about your past relationships, including the existence of any children, legitimate or not. There also may be questions about the financial situation of your future spouse. Even though you may not have full knowledge of your partner's situation, do your best to provide as much accurate information as possible.

Be Accurate

Make sure the information you've given to your lawyer is complete and correct. If it is incomplete, it will cost you. If you forget to list an important asset, you will need to call your lawyer with the information. You will be billed for the telephone call, and if your lawyer has begun work on your agreement, you will be billed for the time needed to make revisions. On the other hand, if you provide incorrect information, the mistake may turn up later on. This may result in additional legal fees when you are forced to litigate the validity of the agreement. An agreement that is declared invalid may cost you thousands of dollars.

Talk to the Secretary

If you must call your lawyer to give additional information or check up on the progress of your agreement, ask to speak with the secretary first. The secretary is probably working on your agreement with your attorney and can forward a message or answer a question for you at no cost.

If you feel that you must speak directly to your attorney, and you have more than one question, jot down your questions before you make your telephone call. This will keep the call shorter. Write the answers next to them and refer to them later.

Keep Files

Keep a file on the progress of your agreement. Put a copy of the information you give to your attorney in it. Keep your meeting and telephone notes in the file and include the dates the conversations took place. You can refer to it before calling your attorney with questions. The answers may already be at your fingertips. Always take your file with you to your attorney's office.

CHAPTER 15
Your Attorney

The most important rule to remember in working with your attorney, and one you have seen before in this book, is to be honest and open at all times. You're hiring someone to draft a very sensitive and personal document that may affect the rest of your life. Some of the issues may be a bit embarrassing to you personally. You must realize, however, that you have asked your attorney to draft the best and most complete document possible. He or she cannot do this without your complete cooperation, openness, and truthfulness.

Your attorney is representing your interests and must respect them. He or she will not and should not judge or criticize your reasons for wanting to draft a prenuptial agreement. In addition, your attorney is not allowed to discuss anything you reveal with anyone other than yourself, not even your partner. Therefore, full disclosure can only benefit you. If you fabricate or leave something out, it may cause problems later.

Sometimes in a lawyer-client relationship, it may seem that the lawyer is the one in charge. If you let your attorney have control you may end up with an agreement that does not exactly fit your needs. To work together effectively, you must be assertive. You must let your lawyer know that you have done your homework and you are to be consulted on each substantial provision. This way, your relationship becomes a partnership of mutual cooperation and respect, and you benefit by creating a comprehensive agreement.

Don't deliberately ignore your attorney's advice. This doesn't necessarily mean that you have to take his or her advice at each and every turn, but only that you think about it, discuss it with whomever you wish, and then make your own decision. If you prefer the advice of your second cousin instead, then you may be spending lots of money for professional work that you might be better able to deliver yourself.

Keep in contact with your attorney's office. If negotiations are taking place between your attorney and your partner's attorney, copies of all documents and correspondence should be sent to you. Keeping in contact does not mean calling your attorney constantly. It does, however, mean being made aware of all developments on a regular and routine basis.

What to Tell Your Attorney

Explain your reasons for having a prenuptial agreement prepared. Do you want children from a prior marraige to be provided for? Do you want family wealth to remain intact and not be dissipated? Do you want to claim future assets for yourself? The attorney must know your motivations before he or she can begin molding an agreement to suit your needs.

Are you using your prenuptial agreement as a tool to plan your estate in the event of your death? Are you more interested in creating a document that will address the distribution of your assets, should a divorce take place? You will want to make sure that the prenuptial agreement does not conflict with your will. If you have had a will prepared, give it to your attorney.

You should tell your lawyer about any previous marriages and all children you have had, regardless of whether the children were legitimate or whether you have custody of them.

You must completely disclose your finances to your attorney, whether or not certain income appears in your federal or state income tax returns. Remember, your attorney cannot divulge any of this information. If you believe for any reason that you cannot trust your attorney with confidential information, you may want to discuss your apprehension. If you feel this is not possible, you should consider choosing another attorney.

What Not to Tell Your Attorney

Don't waste time discussing matters that have no bearing on the preparation of your agreement. More than likely, you will be paying your lawyer on an hourly basis, so stay on the subject. Wandering off may be extremely expensive.

If you have been divorced, you should bring your divorce decree to your work session. Don't spend excessive time discussing the details of the divorce if you have the final judgment in hand. Your lawyer must take a look at the terms of the decree, but he can't change it.

There's no need to discuss your present, past, or future sex life or whom you voted for in the last election. There's absolutely no need to discuss anything with your attorney other than information pertinent to your financial situation and relevant to the agreement you wish drafted.

What to Hide from Your Attorney

Anything you hide from your attorney may come back to haunt you in the future. Revising the document will only cost you time, money, and perhaps a bit of embarrassment. On a much more serious level, failure to fully disclose all relevant information may result in the voiding of your prenuptial agreement somewhere down the road, when you need its protection the most. Again, if you feel you cannot trust your attorney, you should not be using that attorney.

What to Ask Your Attorney

You must ask your attorney to explain the law in your state regarding prenuptial agreements and any tax implications. Make sure to ask about any clause you are not absolutely sure of in the draft of the agreement. You should look over the agreement provision by provision when it is presented to you completely. You should know the meaning of each provision. Make sure that you have asked your attorney to explain the impact of your agreement as a whole. It is your lawyer's responsibility to draft the document in accordance with your desires and with the laws of the state in which you plan to marry and reside. It is your responsibility to ask your attorney about anything you do not understand.

Make sure you *ask before you sign* your agreement; failure to ask may cost you greatly in the future. Once it is signed, you are charged with knowledge of the agreement and you will not be able to tell a court you did not understand it.

What Not to Ask Your Attorney

Your attorney is not a marriage counselor or in the business of making personal decisions on your behalf. Do not ask your attorney whether you should leave your family heirlooms to your wife or sister. This puts your attorney in the position of making your personal decisions and if they turn out to be bad ones, there will be bad feelings.

Getting a Second Opinoin

Whether or not it is important for you to get a second opinion depends on the confidence you have in the lawyer you have chosen. It also depends on the confidence you have gained by reading this book. It is not unusual for a client to seek a second opinion when he is unsure of the manner in which an attorney is handling his case. A second opinion is often sought in complex litigation and divorce matters.

It would not be unusual to ask another attorney to review the document your attorney of choice has prepared for you. A second opinion can be rendered relatively quickly by another attorney at small cost and no harm to you.

Get a second opinion if you believe that the document your attorney has drafted for you is flawed in some way, but express your concerns to your attorney before seeking any other advice. If you are unsatisfied with the response, then, by all means, review the document with another lawyer before you sign it.

You might also get a second opinion if the lawyer who drafted your agreement left out something you wanted included. If this second attorney is indeed knowledgeable, then tell him about the clause and your lawyer's reason for omitting it. You must be completely truthful with this new attorney and make sure that he knows all the facts and circumstances surrounding the controversy; if he is not able to accurately assess your situation, you may end up with an unenforceable agreement.

Using the Same Attorney

It is extremely unwise to use one attorney to draft the prenuptial agreement for both of you. Be very leery of any attorney who suggests that he or she can adequately represent both parties. It would be a clear conflict of interest and the agreement would be declared null and void.

More and more state courts are making determinations that a prenuptial agreement is invalid because one of the parties failed to have adequate independent legal representation. The value of legal representation for each of the parties independent of the other cannot be underestimated where the ultimate validity of the agreement is concerned. Get your own lawyer. Make sure your spouse or intended spouse gets his or her own lawyer.

Even if you are the one who has arranged to have the prenuptial agreement drawn up, you must insist and require that your spouse-to-be chooses an attorney on his or her own to review and discuss the agreement. Failure to have each party represented by counsel can be disastrous in the long run.

Timetable of Events

Once your intended agrees to the idea of a prenuptial agreement (which could take a long time), approximately three or four months should be allotted to finalize the agreement.

Because you are the one who initiated the idea, take the lead in having the agreement drawn up by visiting your own attorney's office.

Once you have your meeting, the lawyer will be left to formalize the agreement. It will probably take two to three weeks to adequately review your documents and incorporate your requests into an appropriate agreement. Then there will be another meeting with your attorney where you will review the agreement.

Once this is completed, your intended and your intended's attorney should receive copies of the agreement for review. Then the attorneys will contact each other to iron out any problems. This will take approximately two to three weeks.

After these initial discussions, you are ready for the first four-way meeting of the two lawyers and the two "lovebirds." This should be a low-key meeting to discuss any remaining problems.

Once you do this, one of the attorneys, probably the initiating spouse's attorney, should take the paperwork back to his or her office for the final draft. This should take a week to ten days, depending on the complexity of the agreement.

After this is completed and reviewed by all parties, you are ready for the final signing. This will take place in one of the attorney's offices with everyone present. Once the agreement is signed, copies will be made for everyone, including you, your partner, and each attorney.

The agreement will be effective on the date of your marriage, or if you are already married, on the date you mutually agree upon.

CHAPTER 16
Case Histories

In order to give you a better perspective of prenuptial and post-nuptial agreements, these actual case histories deal with a mixture of problems and refer you to specific wording in the sample agreements. They start with a simple situation and progress in complexity. Names have been changed to protect all concerned.

Case I

Dr. Richard Jones, age fifty-nine, would very much like to marry a fifty-eight-year-old nurse whom he has been dating for three months. He has been warned by his friends that she is a gold digger. He has never been married before, is in love for the first time in his life, and has no children. Dr. Jones is worth approximately $2.5 million, which includes the value of his medical practice.

Nurse Gold has been married three times, twice to doctors. She has five children by these marriages and all of them are over age twenty-one. Nurse Gold has virtually no assets except a small pension. Both parties are healthy.

Analysis

This is a fairly simple situation: the gold-digger problem. Dr. Jones wishes to marry for love, knowing that Nurse Gold is not marrying him for his money. He does not have to provide for any prior wives or children, and he does not have to provide for Nurse Gold's children, because they are over age twenty-one. He simply wants to keep his own assets and property free of any claims by Nurse Gold.

The situation is probably best dealt with by utilizing the short-form prenuptial agreement on page 117. Certain deletions concerning Nurse Gold's children would be easily made so that Dr. Jones will not need to support them.

Case II

Susan Halley, age twenty-seven, wishes to marry Jim Sanders, age thirty-two. She is the widow of Richard Halley, a computer genius who struck it rich developing computer systems. Halley died three years ago, leaving an estate of approximately $6 million, Susan, and two very young children.

Sanders, an accountant, has a total net worth of approximately $500,000. He and Susan plan to marry and have more children. Jim also plans to adopt Susan's two children.

Susan is reasonably sure that Jim is marrying her for love, not money. She would also like to provide for her present children's future.

Analysis

This is a slightly more complex situation than the first. The gold-digging problem may be present but we are not even reasonably sure of it. The additional problem is the children. How present and future children are to be provided for must be decided now.

The problem of the children is not that complex because Susan is the natural parent. Her only problem is in providing for the children equally and retaining control over her assets.

The short-form prenuptial agreement, with some additions, can provide the answers. The short-form agreement allows Susan to provide for her present and future children by a will. In addition, because of Jim's earning potential, Susan may want her adopted children to have the right to inherit Jim's property and to receive specific sums of money accumulated during her first marriage in the event of her death. Including paragraphs on pages 164, 168 and 169, concerning the adoption and providing for children of prior marriages, can clarify these requirements.

Case III

Robin Morley Eric, the former wife of the president of a large construction company, has been married to Jason Eric for approximately four years. There were no children by either his or her prior marriage. Jason is presently running Robin's company and their marriage is sound and prosperous.

Robin and Jason had agreed orally, but not in writing, before marriage to have a prenuptial arrangement. They now wish to put it in writing.

Analysis

This is once again a relatively simple situation, which can be solved by using the short-form prenuptial agreement. Delete some inapplicable paragraphs, add the postnuptial ratification of the oral antenuptial agreement on page 174, and you have a viable agreement.

Case IV

Andrew Frank, age forty-seven, father of seven- and nine-year-olds, wishes to marry Julie Allison, age forty-eight, mother of two children. Julie's children are ages twenty-one, a junior in college, and twenty-three, employed by a large corporation.

Andrew's former wife will not consent to Julie adopting her children. But Andrew, of course, does wish to provide for them and insure their future the same way Julie wishes to insure her own children's future. Although Andrew and Julie are both wealthy, both feel that theirs is a marriage of love. They wish to avoid fighting over division of property should they ever divorce. Both parties are healthy and employed.

Analysis

With a lack of consent by Andrew's ex-wife, there is little or no chance in most states of Julie adopting Andrew's children. However, if the ex-wife dies, Julie may wish to adopt them. Provisions for their inheriting Julie's estate can be made now, contingent on death or demise of their natural mother, by using the adoption paragraphs on page 164.

Andrew and Julie should also consider using the paragraphs establishing separate property found on page 106. Because they both seem to be marrying for love, they might be interested in transferring their property upon death (page 144) or establishing trust funds for surviving spouses (page 147) as well as including life insurance provisions (page 153).

The major concerns here are the care of Andrew's children and Julie's junior in college. The minor children can be taken care of by the support of minors paragraph (page 162). The college student can be taken care of by using the same paragraphs, with minor changes, or by creating a trust fund prior to the marriage.

Case V

Kari Bunks, sixty-three years old, has three children by a prior marriage. She has a net worth of approximately $2 million. She wishes to marry David Donald, a widower, age sixty-five, with two children. All five children are over age twenty-one with families of their own.

Kari has a net estate of approximately $300,000. She has a nice income from social security and her pension. She wishes to provide for herself if David predeceases her, and she also wishes to help her children.

David is worth $5 million, and wishes to provide for his children and grandchildren. David is not well and, unlike Kari, does not have continued health insurance through his prior employment.

Both of the parties admit that this is a marriage of companionship. David is willing to make economic concessions to Kari so that everybody's needs are fulfilled.

Analysis

Marriages of companionship are generally the easiest to deal with. Both parties are generally friends and realize that there is a business, as well as a personal aspect, to the agreement. The long-form prenuptial agreement should be utilized (page 103). You need to consider the establishment of the support rights on death or termination of marriage (pages 104 and 107), establishment of separate property (pages 104 and 106), marital property (pages 106), and rights of inheritance (page 108). You might wish to include a transfer of some property on the death of one of the spouses (page 144) or a trust fund for Kari (page 147), or annuity (page 151). Life insurance as an answer to Kari's needs and desires may also be included as a possibility (see page 153).

An additional section should be included to require David to acquire and be responsible for health insurance. This paragraph can easily be improvised from the paragraphs that are already given.

Case VI

Lee Samuel has been married to Alix Faith for seven years and had a prenuptial agreement drawn up prior to their marriage. Lee was a former baseball pitcher and still earns money through endorsements. They are not planning to have more children.

Lee now feels that Alix did marry for love, as proved by the birth of his two children and her care of him and his child from a prior marriage.

He wants to do away with the agreement. He feels it is interfering with their relationship. Alix has been pestering him to do it for some time, but in a nice way.

Analysis

What was feared to be marriage for money apparently turned out to be one for love. Lee is a lucky client. A simple document, revocation of postnuptial agreement (see page 139), is all that is needed to accomplish his wishes.

Case VII

Lisa Ann is ninety-three and was married to a past president of a very large corporation. She has been well provided for with stock options, stock, and a large house in Connecticut as well as one on Long Island. Her interest income alone is over $300,000 a year.

She is madly in love with a twenty-seven-year-old man who is a reasonably successful attorney. She has four children, nine grandchildren, and twenty-two great grandchildren. He has one child by a prior marriage, which ended in divorce.

Analysis

This is, of course, a classic situation. No reasonable person is going to believe that this is a marriage-for-love situation although it well may be. Clearly, you must assume the worst and hope for the best. Lisa Ann needs a complete, carefully drawn agreement. The agreement must provide for the unforeseen termination of the marriage by death or divorce. It should utilize the separate property ideas along with definitive clauses concerning support of the parties either during the marriage or after their separation or termination of the relationship. Life insurance provisions should also be considered.

An agreement, which will provide most, if not all, of the provisions necessary, is presented in the sample prenuptial agreement on page 120.

Case VIII

Jim Elliott, age forty-one, wishes to marry Cindy Van, age thirty-nine. Both are college educated. Both have children under age sixteen. Jim is Jewish and Mary is Catholic. Both of their former spouses are alive and well. They want to have a child together and agree upon the religion of the unborn child.

Jim's estate is worth quite a bit more than Cindy's. Jim earns about $125,000 per year. Cindy earns approximately $35,000 per year.

They both agree that the marriage is for love. Both have agreed that they will not impose their religion on the children of their prior marriages and that the children of their prior marriages should be treated equally.

Analysis

This is a very difficult, intricate, and yet classic problem. The most sensitive area is, obviously, the religion problem. Jim and Mary must be able to put their requirements into their agreement with very extensive, specific wording. This should include religious education obligations as well as names of churches or temples to be attended.

Provisions concerning children of a prior marriage (pages 103, 104), support of minors (page 163), death of a natural parent (pages 166, 168, 171), as well as life insurance (page 153) provisions should be considered.

Case IX

George Will is about to get married to Joan Lyon. George is a wealthy doctor. Joan has a good job but is not known for her thriftiness. In fact, Joan's estate shows $10,000 in assets and $35,000 in debts. George would like to hold down Joan's spending to make sure that he does not become responsible for her debts.

Analysis

In most states, debts prior to marriage are those of the person who created them. They are not transferred to the new spouse and, therefore, will not become George's just because he married Joan.

An agreement should be drawn to create a marital property fund (see page 133). This will create a fund for Joan's spending and pay for her debts. There will be provisions for curtailing Joan's spending. Otherwise the other standard provisions in the short-form prenuptial agreement (page 117) are all that is necessary.

CHAPTER 17
Dos and Dont's

DO hire an experienced attorney. You get what you pay for.

DON'T cheat. This can only lead to problems in the future.

DO be sincere. Save irrational behavior for the future. If you are fighting now, maybe you ought to reconsider marriage.

DO be fair to yourself and your partner. You have a lifetime of living together ahead of you. A lack of fair play may erode a good relationship.

DO remember that prenuptial agreements have nothing to do with love. If you maintain your love for each other, there may never be a need to implement the agreement.

DON'T be afraid to ask why your attorney is making certain suggestions, and don't be afraid to ask questions.

DO try to learn something about prenuptial agreements and divorce law on your own. Do a little advance reading before consulting with your attorney.

DON'T make snap decisions. Do not make the determinations in the attorney's office but later, after you have thought about the matter in a nice, calm, quiet, unpressured environment.

DO be prepared for meetings with your attorney. Bring all the financial documents with you.

DO be on time for all your meetings.

DON'T withhold any information. Answer any and all reasonable questions.

DON'T call your attorney every five minutes. Wait until you have accumulated a number of questions, after a reasonable period of time has passed.

CHAPTER 18

Questions and Answers

1. What is a prenuptial agreement?

    A prenuptial agreement is a contract that you hope will never have to be enforced. Sometimes a prenuptial agreement is called an antenuptial agreement or a premarital agreement. It describes how your property and your spouse's will be divided if you are divorced or permanently separated. It also describes how financial support for your children from a prior marriage will be arranged.

2. What is a postnuptial agreement?

    A postnuptial agreement is similar to a prenuptial agreement but is drawn up and signed after marriage.

3. Do I need a prenuptial agreement?

    Most likely. With the extremely high percentage of divorces attending today's marriages, a prenuptial or postnuptial agreement is likely to save you thousands of dollars in attorney's fees and infinite amounts of anxiety and aggravation.

4. Are prenuptial agreements legal in every state?

    Generally they are. Certain requirements differ from state to state. Your attorney knows what the laws are in your state.

5. Do I need a lawyer concerning this agreement?

    You don't necessarily need one, but you should at least consult with an attorney who has drawn up prenuptial agreements and is experienced in divorce work. An attorney knows state and federal tax implications, as well.

6. What should I include in the prenuptial agreement?

    Everything you own and plan to own. For a complete list, see Chapter 11.

7. Do prenuptial agreements have to be in writing?

    Yes, for ancient historical reasons.

8. How do courts look at prenuptial agreements?

    Generally courts look at prenuptial agreements favorably. They do not look favorably, however, on an agreement that promotes separation or divorce.

9. Is a prenuptial agreement and/or postnuptial agreement for everyone?

    If you intend to ever get married or if you are married, an agreement can certainly be of value.

10. How long should a prenuptial or postnuptial agreement be?

    There is no specific length. It can be long or short, depending on your needs. The appendix of this book contains the wording of these agreements.

11. Who can enter into a prenuptial agreement?

    Generally anyone who is competent.

12. Should my partner also have a lawyer?

    Yes. Each partner must give an honest statement of liabilities and assets, and state that each has entered into the agreement voluntarily. Having your own attorney will validate this.

13. A lawyer made up an agreement for a friend of mine. Can I use this agreement?

    You can use the agreement only if your situation is exactly the same. Even so, you should still consult a lawyer to make sure it is appropriate for you.

14. Where can I find a lawyer who knows how to draw up an agreement properly?

    Usually attorneys who do divorce work also do prenuptial agreements. A primary source is through a friend who either had an agreement drawn up or was divorced and was satisfied with the attorney's work.

15. I'm already married. Can I still do an agreement?

    A qualified yes. There are some states that recognize postnuptial agreements.

16. Can you provide for an unborn child in a prenuptial agreement?

    Yes.

17. How important is honesty?

    Of utmost importance. If you are not absolutely candid concerning assets, liabilities, and so forth, you may be accused of fraud and the agreement may be overturned.

18. Is there anything you should leave out of an agreement?

    You might leave out anything that would not or could not be divided during the potential divorce proceeding. Consultation with an attorney should be required to see if your assessment is correct before leaving it out.

19. Is it possible to write an ironclad agreement?

    Unfortunately, nothing is perfect. By consulting with a knowledgeable attorney, you will come close to having an agreement that you want.

20. Is there some way to avoid hiring individual attorneys?

    It is in the best interest of all concerned that both parties have their own attorney.

21. Will my children still be able to inherit my estate?

    Yes, anything you want can be provided for in the agreement.

22. After I sign the agreement, can I change it?

    Only if you both agree to do so.

23. If I want to cancel the agreement entirely, can I do so?

    Only if you both agree to do so.

24. Is there any part of the agreement that cannot be changed?

    Probably not, but it depends on the individual state.

25. If my fiancé and I sign an agreement and decide not to get married, is either party bound by the agreement?

    Generally not. The agreement comes into effect only when and if it is signed and if marriage actually takes place.

26. How many copies of the prenuptial agreement should there be?

    There should be at least four copies of the agreement. One copy is yours, one is your spouse's, and the others are for your individual attorneys. Each copy should have original signatures and be considered original documents.

27. Should you tell your friends or family about a prenuptial agreement?

    As with a will, there is no necessity to advise anybody of anything. You may wish to notify someone other than your attorney of the prenuptial agreement so that person might cause its provisions to be implemented should you die.

28. Can a will do the same thing as a prenuptial agreement without the expense?

   Generally not. In many states the individual laws of that state allow the surviving spouse to "take against the will" or renounce the will. This can lessen the possibility that all of the desires of the will maker will be carried out. A will should be considered with a prenuptial agreement.

29. How much does a prenuptial agreement cost?

   It depends on whether your attorney charges an hourly rate or a flat fee. It also depends on his experience, and the preparation you have put into it yourself.

30. Are there any states where prenuptial agreements are illegal?

   Not at this time, but prenuptial agreements are certainly frowned upon in a few states.

31. How much should you be worth before you get a prenuptial agreement?

   A prenuptial agreement doesn't depend on the amount of money that you have. It's only suggested that the more money you have, the more need there is for an agreement. If neither of you have any money, an agreement may not be necessary.

32. When do you not need to enter into a prenuptial agreement?
   When you're not getting married.

APPENDIX: MODEL AGREEMENTS AND PARAGRAPHS

COMPLETE
AGREEMENTS

LONG-FORM PRENUPTIAL AGREEMENT

The forms and paragraphs on pages 103–112 comprise a prenuptial agreement and define the rights of the parties. They are written in general terms to meet the requirements of most, but not necessarily all, states.

There is a section where the type, extent, and probable value of the assets and property of the parties involved can be defined. In most jurisdictions and states, each party to a prenuptial agreement must make a complete and full disclosure of his and her finances, which means his and her assets and debts. Generally there should be a full and general disclosure of all "situations" to assure the fairness of the agreement at the time of the signing. Not to disclose everything would increase the possibility of the agreement's being voided by a court of law at a later date.

The reader may treat these pages and paragraphs as a supermarket of ideas in which he or she can shop for specifics that fulfill individual needs and requirements. The following is not meant to obviate the need to hire an attorney. Only by consultation with an experienced attorney can one hope to comply with the individual requirements of prenuptial agreements in each state.

LONG-FORM PRENUPTIAL AGREEMENT

Prepared by: _____ *(signature)*

(typed name)

This Agreement is entered into on_____ *(date)* between _____ *(name of future husband)*(Husband), residing at_____*(address)* _____(County),_____(State), and _____ *(name of future wife)* (Wife), residing at _____*(address)*, _____(County), _____(State). These individuals are collectively referred to as the "Parties." The Parties intend to be married on _____*(date)* at _____ *(location)*. This Agreement will be effective on _____*(the specific date of the marriage)*.

ARTICLE 1. PURPOSES

(Select appropriate paragraphs)

Intent to Define Property Rights

1.01. The Parties to this Agreement intend to define their respective rights in the property of the other during marriage, and to avoid interests that they might acquire in the property of the other as incidents of their marriage relationship if it were not for the operation of this Agreement.

Intent to Provide for Children of Former Marriage

1.02. The Parties desire to provide for the support of the _____(child *or* children) of _____(the Husband *or* Wife *or* both Parties) by a former marriage, until _____(this child *or* these children) _____ *(specify condition, e.g.,* reach the age of eighteen *or* graduate from college). The names and ages of _____(this child *or* each child) are set forth in Paragraph 2.01 of this Agreement.

103

Intent to Establish Rights on Death

1.03. The Parties desire to establish the rights of each to inherit from the other in the event of the death of either.

Intent to Establish Property Rights on Termination

1.04. The Parties enter into this Agreement and into marriage with the intention that their marriage shall endure until death. However, in recognition of the reality that due to circumstances unforeseen or unknown at this time that marriage could be terminated by divorce or permanent separation, the Parties intend by this Agreement to establish their respective rights in all property if the marriage is terminated. The Parties intend to set forth criteria by which property may be classified as separate property or as marital property, recognizing that these criteria are in variance from those likely to be applied by a court of law in absence of this Agreement. The Parties do this with the intention of removing property that would otherwise be divisible from the application of equitable distribution (community property distribution) in the event of termination of the marriage.

Intent to Establish Support Rights on Termination

1.05. In further recognition of the possible but unforeseen termination of the marriage, the Parties intend to determine the obligation of each to support the other on divorce or permanent separation. *(Add if applicable:* Each party will enter the marriage fully capable of providing for his or her own support. Each possesses significant separate economic resources and has significant income-earning potential. Neither anticipates that during the course of the marriage there will be any change in the capacity of either to provide completely for his or her own support. For these reasons, the Parties intend by this Agreement to permanently waive the right to seek support in any form from the other in the event the marriage is terminated.)

ARTICLE 2. RECITALS

Children by a Former Marriage

2.01. Husband is the father of the following children by a former marriage:_____ *(specify, e.g.,* _____[*name*],

a boy, _____ years old; _____ [*name*],
a girl, _____ years old). Wife is the mother of the
following children by a former marriage: _____ *(spec-*
ify, e.g., _____ [*name*], a girl, _____ years old).

Representation by Independent Counsel

2.02. Husband and Wife acknowledge that each has been represented by independent counsel in the negotiation of this Agreement;
that counsel representing each party was of the party's own choosing;
that each party has read the Agreement and has had the meaning and
legal consequences of the Agreement explained by his or her counsel;
and that each party elects, on advice of his or her independent
counsel, to enter into this legally binding contract.

Disclosure of Property

2.03. Each party to this Agreement has given the other a full and
complete disclosure of the assets, income, and other property of the
party or the party's estate. A list of the assets, income, and property
of Husband and his estate is attached as Exhibit A and incorporated
by reference. A list of the assets, income, and property of the Wife and
her estate is attached as Exhibit B and incorporated by reference.

It is understood that the figures and amounts contained in Exhibit
A and Exhibit B are approximately correct and not necessarily exact.

The estimated gross value of the assets and property of the
Husband is approximately $_____, not including house-
hold goods, automobiles, and miscellaneous items not to exceed
$_____, and the total indebtedness of Husband is ap-
proximately $_____, leaving an estimated net value of
$_____.

The estimated gross value of the assets and property of Wife is
approximately $_____, not including household goods,
automobiles, and miscellaneous items not to exceed
$_____, and the total indebtedness of Wife is approxi-
mately $_____, leaving an estimated net value of
$_____.

Consideration

2.04. This agreement is made in consideration of the marriage,
and in consideration of the mutual promises granting to each party

_____ *(specify, e.g.,* the right to acquire separate property during marriage, the right to dispose of his or her estate free from claims from the other party, and the right to be free from claims for an equitable [equal or community property division] division of property and for support in the event of the termination of the marriage).

ARTICLE 3. AGREEMENTS

Establishment of Separate Property

3.01. Except as otherwise provided in this Agreement, the assets, income, and property of the Parties listed in this Agreement as Exhibits A and B *(add if desired:)*, together with all income and increases in value arising from that property during marriage regardless of the reason for the income or increase,) shall be owned as the separate property of that party during marriage. All property that either party may acquire by way of gift or inheritance, whether under a will or by intestate distribution, is similarly the separate property of the owner-party. *(Add if desired:* All wages, salary, and income of each party earned or received during marriage, together with all property purchased with such wages, salary, and income, shall also be the separate property of that party.)

Treatment of Separate Property

3.02. Each party shall have the absolute and unrestricted right to manage, control, dispose of, or otherwise deal with his or her separate property free from any claim that may be made by the other party by reason of their marriage, and with the same effect as if no marriage had been consummated between them. By this Agreement, each party waives, discharges, and releases all right, title, and interest in and to the separate property that the other party now owns or acquires after the execution of this Agreement, or acquires from the proceeds of any separate property now owned.

(Add if desired:)
Marital Property

3.03. During the course of the marriage the Parties shall make equal periodic contributions to a fund for the maintenance of their household and the care and support of the children of the marriage.

All property purchased with the proceeds of this fund shall be deemed marital property. Each party shall have equal rights in regard to the management of and disposition of all marital property.

Disposition of Property on Termination of Marriage

3.04. If the marriage should terminate for any reason other than the death of a party, and without regard to the fault of either party in causing the termination, all property as set forth in Exhibits A and B to this Agreement, and all separate property as set forth in Paragraph 3.01 of this Agreement, shall remain the separate property of the respective Parties, and neither shall claim or have any right to compel the equitable distribution (equal or community property distribution) of any separate property. All marital property shall be subject to a just and equitable distribution (community property or equal distribution) between the Parties.

(If lump sum is to be transferred, add the following provision:)
Transfer of Lump Sum to Future Spouse

3.05. Within _____ days after their marriage, _____ *(name of payor spouse)* agrees to pay _____ *(name of payee spouse)* the sum of $_____; this sum to be _____(his *or* her) separate property.

Support and Maintenance of Children

3.06. _____(Husband *or* Wife) agrees to provide for the support of the children of _____(Wife *or* Husband) by a former marriage, until they _____ *(specify condition, e.g.,* reach the age of eighteen *or* graduate from college), for as long as the Parties are married. The names and ages of these children are set forth in Paragraph 2.01 of this Agreement.

(Include if desired:)
Support of Parties on Termination of Marriage

3.07. If the marriage should terminate for any reason, and without regard to the fault of either party in causing the termination, each party agrees to be solely responsible for his or her own future support after termination, regardless of any unforeseen change in circumstances or economic condition or well-being. By this provision, the Parties intend to permanently waive all rights to alimony, spousal support, or post-divorce payments of any kind from one party for the support of the other. Nothing in this provision is intended to in any way affect the rights of any minor children of the marriage to the support of both Parties.

(Add if desired:)
Rights of Inheritance

3.08. Except as set forth in this Paragraph, each party waives and renounces any right to inherit from the other, whether by intestacy, or pursuant to statute or rule of law. _____(*Set forth provisions regarding inheritance, e.g.,* Each party agrees to execute a will contemporaneously with the execution of this agreement establishing a testamentary trust naming the other as sole beneficiary. Each trust shall have a corpus consisting of property from the estate of the deceased spouse worth at least $100,000. Each party agrees not to revoke his or her will except pursuant to a mutual revocation.)

Release of Each Party
from All Other Claims and Liabilities

3.09. Each party agrees to release the other party from all claims and liabilities, except as specified in this Agreement. Neither of the Parties to this Agreement shall be responsible for the debts of the other party that have accumulated up to the time of the signing of this Agreement, and neither of the Parties shall be responsible for any debts contracted after the signing of this Agreement unless both Parties have agreed to assume these debts.

Agreement to Join in Execution of Other Instruments

3.10. Both Parties covenant that they shall willingly, at the request of either party—or his or her successor or assigns—execute, deliver, and properly acknowledge whatever additional instruments may be required to carry out the intention of this Agreement, and shall execute, deliver, and properly acknowledge any deeds or other documents so that good and marketable title to any property can be conveyed by one party free from any claim of the other party.

ARTICLE 4. TERMS AND CONDITIONS OF AGREEMENT

Agreement Conditioned on Marriage

4.01. This Agreement is entered into assuming that the Parties are to be married, and its effectiveness is expressly conditioned on the marriage between the Parties actually taking place. If, for any reason, the marriage is not consummated, the Agreement will be of no force or effect.

Duty to Support Children of this Marriage

4.02. Nothing contained in this Agreement shall be construed as absolving either party of his or her statutory duty to support any minor children of the marriage and to provide them with an education suitable to that party's circumstances.

Entirety

4.03. This Agreement contains the entire understanding of the parties, and no representations or promises have been made except as contained in this Agreement.

Severability

4.04. If any term, provision, covenant, or condition of this Agreement is held by a court of competent jurisdiction to be invalid, void, or unenforceable, the remainder of the provisions shall remain in full force and effect and shall in no way be affected, impaired, or invalidated.

Effect of Divorce or Separation

4.05. Each of the Parties by the execution of this Agreement intends that the provisions of this Agreement shall be binding on each of them and their heirs in the event of a divorce or separation by and between the parties.

No Limitation on Inter Vivos Transfers

4.06. Nothing in this Agreement shall affect the right of either party voluntarily to transfer real or personal property to the other party, or the right to receive property transferred by the other party, during their lifetime.

No Limitation on Testamentary Transfers

4.07. Nothing in this Agreement shall affect the right of either party to devise or bequeath property to the other party in excess of that required by this Agreement. Nothing in this Agreement shall be construed as a waiver or renunciation of the right of either party to take under the last will of the other.

Persons Bound

4.08. The Parties and their respective heirs, devisees, legatees, personal representatives, guardians, successors in interest, and assigns shall be bound by the provisions of this Agreement.

Waiver of Breach and Subsequent Breaches

4.09. Waiver of any breach of this Agreement does not constitute approval or waiver of subsequent breaches.

Amendments and Modifications

4.10. Amendments and modifications of this Agreement must be written and executed in the same manner as this Agreement.

Agreement Governed by Laws of _____

4.11. This Agreement is to be governed by the laws of the State of _____

IN WITNESS WHEREOF, the Parties have executed this Agreement on the day and year first written above.

_____ *(signature)*
(typed name of future husband)

_____ *(signature)*
(typed name of future wife)

(Add if agreement is to be recorded:)
ACKNOWLEDGMENT

STATE OF _____
COUNTY OF_____

I certify that on this _____ *(date)*, Husband and Wife each personally appeared before me and severally acknowledged under oath, to my satisfaction, that they are the persons named in this

Agreement and the persons who executed this Agreement, and that they each signed, sealed, and delivered the same as each party's act and deed for the purposes expressed in the Agreement.

_____ *(signature)*
Notary Public

(Notarial Seal)

Notary Public for the
State of _____
My Commission Expires:
_____ *(date)*

(Optional certifications of attorney for future husband:)
CERTIFICATION OF ATTORNEY

I hereby certify that I am an attorney-at-law, duly licensed and admitted to practice in the State of _____; that I have been employed by _____ *(name of future husband)*, a party to this Agreement; that I have advised him with respect to the Agreement and explained to him the meaning and legal effect of it; and that Husband has acknowledged his full and complete understanding of this Agreement and its legal consequences, and has freely and voluntarily executed the Agreement in my presence.
Date:_____

_____ *(signature)*
(typed name), Attorney for Husband

(Optional certification of attorney for future wife:)
CERTIFICATION OF ATTORNEY

I hereby certify that I am an attorney-at-law, duly licensed and admitted to practice in the State of _____; that I have been employed by _____ *(name of future wife)*, a party to this Agreement; that I have advised her with respect to this Agreement and explained to her the meaning and legal effect of it; and that Wife has acknowledged her full and complete understanding of this Agreement and its legal consequences, and has

111

freely and voluntarily executed the Agreement in my presence.
Date:_____

_____ *(signature)*
(typed name), Attorney for Wife

EXHIBIT A

Schedule of Assets, Income, and Property of Husband and his estate as of _____*(date)*.

Assets	Value
_____	_____
_____	_____
_____	_____

Property	Value
_____	_____
_____	_____
_____	_____

Source of Income	Amount of Income
_____	_____
_____	_____
_____	_____

EXHIBIT B

Schedule of Assets, Income, and Property of Wife and her estate as of _____*(date)*.

(See EXHIBIT A, above, for schedule form.)

PRENUPTIAL AGREEMENT TO IDENTIFY SEPARATE PROPERTY BROUGHT INTO MARRIAGE

The following agreement is useful for parties who have a great deal of wealth and wish to identify their individual property that they anticipate taking into the marriage. There are certain provisions concerning inheriting from the other party under a will, which is protection for children and other potential heirs of the individual persons involved.

The one shortcoming of this agreement is that it does not deal with increased value of property brought into the marriage. This, of course, can be dealt with by other paragraphs in other sections of this appendix.

PRENUPTIAL AGREEMENT

This Agreement is entered into on _____ *(date)*, between _____ *(name of husband)* (Husband), residing at _____ *(address)*, _____County, _____State, and _____ *(name of wife)* (Wife), residing at _____ *(address)*, _____County, _____State. These individuals are collectively referred to as the "Parties."

ARTICLE 1. PURPOSE

Intent to Define Property Rights

1.01. The Parties to this Agreement intend to define their separate property as of the date of marriage, and to clarify that neither will obtain any interest in the specified separate property of the other as a result of the marriage.

ARTICLE 2. RECITALS

Representation by Independent Counsel

2.01. Husband and Wife acknowledge that each has been represented by independent counsel in the negotiation of this Agreement; that counsel representing each party was of the party's own choosing; that each party has read the Agreement and has had the meaning and legal consequences of the Agreement explained to him or her by counsel; and that each party elects, on advice of his or her independent counsel, to enter into this legally binding contract.

Disclosure of Property
(Include one of the following provisions.)

2.02. Each party to this Agreement has given the other a full and complete disclosure of the assets, income, and other property of the party or the party's estate. A list of the assets, income, and property of Husband and his estate is attached as Exhibit A and incorporated by reference. A list of the assets, income, and property of Wife is attached as Exhibit B and incorporated by reference. It is understood that the figures and amounts contained in Exhibit A and Exhibit B

114

are approximately correct and not necessarily exact.

The estimated gross value of the assets and property of Husband is approximately $_____, not including household goods, automobiles, and miscellaneous items not to exceed $_____, and the total indebtedness of Husband is approximately $_____, leaving an estimated net value of $_____.

The estimated gross value of the assets and property of Wife is approximately $_____, not including household goods, automobiles, and miscellaneous items not to exceed $_____, and the total indebtedness of Wife is approximately $_____, leaving an estimated net value of $_____.

ARTICLE 3. AGREEMENT

Mutual Release

3.01. The Parties mutually agree that each Party waives, discharges, and releases all claims and rights, actual, inchoate, or contingent, in law and equity, that he or she may acquire in the separately owned property of the other by reason of the Parties' marriage, including but not limited to the following:

(1) The right to have any of the specified separate property made subject to equitable distribution in the event the marriage is terminated other than by the death of one of the Parties;

(2) The rights or claims of dower, curtesy, or any statutory substitutes for these rights and claims as provided by the statutes of the state in which the Parties or either one of them may die domiciled or in which they may own real property;

(3) Either Party's right of election to take against the will of the other;

(4) Either Party's right to a distributive share in the estate of the other should he or she die intestate;

(5) Either Party's right to act as an administrator of the estate of the other;

(6) _____(*Other rights, e.g.,* the right to claim that rents or profits of the separately owned property of either party are community property.)

115

IN WITNESS WHEREOF, the Parties have executed this Agreement on the date first written above.

_____ *(signature)*
(typed name of future husband)

_____ *(signature)*
(typed name of future wife)

(For exhibits listing property, acknowledgment, and certification of attorneys for future spouses, see pages 110–112.)

SHORT-FORM PRENUPTIAL AGREEMENT

The following is a short-form of prenuptial, antenuptial property agreement. Depending on the needs of the reader or writer of this agreement, it might be utilized between parties whose financial situation is relatively simple.

This simple form can be further shortened by deleting some of the *whereas* clauses as well as the paragraphs that might not apply. Before entering into such a short agreement in your individual state, be sure to check the legality of it. Make sure all the necessary paragraphs are intact.

SHORT-FORM PRENUPTIAL AGREEMENT

THIS AGREEMENT made this _____ day of _____, 19_____ between JOHN SMITH, residing at _____ *(street),* _____ *(city),* _____ *(state)* and JANE DOE, residing at _____ _____ *(street),* _____ *(city),* _____ *(state).*

W I T N E S S E T H

WHEREAS, the parties hereto contemplate marriage to each other, and wish to provide for their respective children of their previous marriages; and

WHEREAS, both parties desire to accept the provisions of this Agreement in lieu of all rights which either of them would otherwise acquire, by reason of the contemplated marriage, in the property or estate of the other; and

WHEREAS, each party has fully disclosed to the other the extent and approximate present value of all his or her property and all of the rights and privileges in and to such property; and

WHEREAS, the parties elect, upon advice of independent legal counsel, to enter into a legal binding contract;

NOW, THEREFORE, in consideration of the mutual promises and agreements set forth therein, the parties agree as follows:

1. (a) The items set forth on Schedule A annexed hereto are owned by the respective parties. Insofar as dollar valuations have been assigned to any item, the parties accept such valuation as correct.

(b) Schedule A purports to be as comprehensive as possible. If either party discovers, after the signing of this Agreement, that he or she has omitted any Separate Property, he or she shall promptly notify the other party in writing, and an addendum will be made to Schedule A.

(c) The parties shall have the right to make changes in their Separate Property, by sale, exchange, or other method. In such event the party making such change shall notify the other party, and an addendum will be made to Schedule A reflecting such change.

(d) Each party shall, during his or her lifetime, keep and retain sole ownership, enjoyment, control, and power of disposal of all property listed on Schedule A, ("Separate Property") as owned by such party, free and clear of any title, interest, rights, or claims of the other.

(e) Neither party shall have or establish or make claim to any title, interest, rights, or claims, in the Separate Property of the other, other than as donee or beneficiary under a written document.

2. In the event of the death of either party or in any action by either party for support, and/or maintenance, or separation or divorce arising out of the contemplated marriage, neither party shall have or seek to establish any title, interest, rights, or claims in the Separate Property of the other.

3. Both parties hereby waive the right to act as administrator, administratrix, executor, or executrix of the other's Will, but this waiver shall not prohibit such appointment by duly executed written document.

4. Any increment or increase in value of the Separate Property shall belong to the party owning such Separate Property at the time of the contemplated marriage.

5. Any income earned by either party during the marriage, whether earned for the payment of services rendered, or as income from the Separate Property, shall be first contributed to the basic expenses of the respective party's children. The balance of such income, after payment of any income taxes due thereon, shall then be contributed to the basic living expenses of the parties.

6. This Agreement is made in the State of _____ and shall be construed, governed, and interpreted in accordance with the laws of the State of _____.

7. This Agreement contains the entire understanding of the parties and no representations or provisions have been made by either party except as contained herein.

IN WITNESS WHEREOF, the parties hereto have hereunto set their hands and seals the date and year first above written.

SIGNED, SEALED, AND DELIVERED
IN THE PRESENCE OF: _____(L.S.)
JOHN SMITH

_____

_____(L.S.)
JANE DOE

SAMPLE PRENUPTIAL AGREEMENT

This is an actual agreement that has been drawn up. It encompasses a number of problems not included in the short-form prenuptial agreement.

Prepared by: _____
(typed name of attorney)

_____
(typed name of attorney)

This Agreement is entered into on _____ *(date)*, between John Smith, residing at _____ *(address)*, and Jane Doe, residing at _____ *(address)*. The individuals are collectively referred to as the "Parties" or singly as "Party." The Parties intend to be married on _____ *(date)* in _____ *(place)*. This Agreement will be effective on _____ *(date)*.

1. The Parties to this Agreement intend to define their respective rights in the property of the other during marriage, and to avoid interests that they might acquire in the property of the other as incident of their marriage relationship if it were not for the operation of this Agreement.

2. The Parties further desire to establish the rights of each to inherit from the other in the event of the death of either.

3. The Parties enter into this Agreement and into marriage with the intention that their marriage shall endure until death. However, in recognition of the reality that due to circumstances unforeseen or unknown at this time, the marriage could be terminated by divorce or separation, the Parties intend by this Agreement to establish their respective rights in all property if the marriage is terminated. The Parties intend to set forth criteria by which property may be classified as separate property or as marital property, recognizing that these criteria might possibly be in variance with those possibly or likely to be applied by a court of law in absence of this Agreement. The Parties do this with the intention of removing property that would otherwise be divisible from the application of equitable distribution in the event of termination of the marriage.

4. In further recognition of the possible but unforeseen termination of the marriage, the Parties intend to determine the obligation of each to support the other on divorce, separation, or permanent separation. Each Party will enter the marriage fully capable of providing for his or her own support. Each possesses significant separate economic resources and has significant income-earning potential. For all of the aforementioned reasons, the Parties intend by this Agreement to permanently waive the right to seek support in any form from the other in the event of a separation or in the event of the termination of the marriage.

5. Husband and Wife acknowledge that each has been represented by independent counsel in the negotiation of this Agreement; that counsel representing each Party was of the Party's own choosing; that each Party has read the Agreement and has had the meaning and legal consequences of the Agreement explained by his or her counsel; and that each Party elects, on the advice of his or her independent counsel, to enter into this legally binding contract voluntarily and without duress or coercion of any kind.

6. Each Party to this Agreement has given the other a full and complete disclosure of the assets, income, and other property of the Party or the Party's estate. A list of the assets, income, and property of the Husband and his estate is attached as Exhibit A and incorporated by reference. A list of the assets, income, and property of the Wife and her estate is attached as Exhibit B and incorporated by reference.

It is understood that the figures and amounts contained in Exhibit A and Exhibit B are approximate and not necessarily exact.

The estimated gross value of the assets and property of the Husband is approximately between $6.3 million and $8.2 million exclusive of household goods, automobiles, and miscellaneous items not to exceed $100,000 and the total indebtedness of the Husband is approximately $100,000, leaving an estimated net value of approximately $6.3 million to $8.2 million.

The estimated gross value of the assets and property of the Wife is approximately between $2 million and $2.5 million, exclusive of household goods, automobiles, and miscellaneous items not to exceed $75,000, and the total indebtedness of the Wife is approximately $50,000, leaving an estimated net value of approximately $2 million to $2.5 million.

7.   This Agreement is made in consideration of the marriage, and in consideration of the mutual promises granting to each Party the right to acquire separate property during the marriage, the right to dispose of his or her estate free from the claims from the other Party, the right to be free from claims for an equitable division of property and for support in the event of the termination of the marriage, and the right to be free from claims for support in the event of a separation by the Parties during the marriage.

8.   Except as otherwise provided in this Agreement, the assets, income, and property of the Parties listed in the respective schedules attached to and made a part of this Agreement, as Exhibits A and B, together with all income and increases in value arising from that property during the marriage regardless of the reason for the income or increase, shall be owned as the separate property of that Party during marriage. All property that either Party may acquire by way of gift or inheritance, whether under a will or by intestate distribution, is similarly the separate property of the owner-party. All wages, salary, and income of each Party earned or received during the marriage, together with all property purchased with such wages, salary, and income, shall also be the separate property of that Party; however, the Husband shall maintain and support the Wife in a reasonable manner provided they remain married and continue to reside together.

9.   Each Party shall have the absolute and unrestricted right to manage, control, dispose of, or otherwise deal with his or her separate property free from any claim that may be made by the other party by reason of their marriage, and with the same effect as if no marriage had been consummated between them. By this Agreement, each Party waives, discharges, and releases all right, title, and interest in and to the separate property now owned.

10.   A.   During the course of the marriage the Parties may but shall not be obligated to make contributions to a fund for the maintenance of their household, or may acquire property in joint names, regardless of the source of the funds, shall be deemed marital property. Each Party shall have equal rights in regard to the management of and disposition of all marital property.

B.   Should the Parties acquire a home during the course of their marriage as Tenants-in-Common, and should the marriage terminate by reason of the death of one of the Parties, then the surviving spouse shall have a life estate in the home with the continuing option, exercisable at any time, to purchase the remaining interest from the estate of the deceased spouse. The purchase price for the deceased spouse's interest in the home shall be the fair market value at the time of the exercise of the option determined by an appraiser appointed by the Judge of the Highest Court in the County in which the home is located or by some other mutually agreeable method.

C. Should the marriage terminate by reason of separation or divorce, then no life estate shall exist for either Party and the home shall be considered marital property as previously defined and shall be distributed accordingly.

D. Any contribution to the day to day maintenance of the house or the household shall not serve to increase either Party's equity interest in the home.

11. If the marriage should terminate for any reason or for no reason whatsoever and without regard to the fault of either Party in causing the termination, or in the event of a separation, all property as set forth in Exhibits A and B of this Agreement, and all separate property as set forth in Paragraph 8 of this Agreement, shall remain the separate property of the respective Parties, and neither shall claim or have any right to compel the equitable distribution of any separate property. All marital property as referred to in paragraph 10 of this Agreement shall be subject to equal, as opposed to equitable, distribution between the Parties.

12. If the marriage should terminate, or should the Parties separate, for any reason and without regard to the fault of either party in causing the termination or separation, each Party agrees to be solely responsible for his or her own future support after termination or separation, regardless of any unforeseen change in circumstances or economic condition or well-being. By this provision, the Parties intend to permanently waive all rights to alimony, pendente lite alimony, pendente lite support, spousal support, or post-divorce payments of any kind from one Party for the support of the other.

13. Subject to paragraph 21, each Party waives and renounces any right to inherit from the other, whether by intestacy, or pursuant to statute or rule of law, or pursuant to case law. Each Party may determine how the entirety of his or her separate property shall be

distributed at the time of his or her death by his or her own Last Will.

14. Each Party agrees to release the other Party from all claims and liabilities, except as specified in this Agreement. Neither of the Parties to this Agreement shall be responsible for the debts of the other Party that have accumulated up to the time of the signing of this Agreement, and neither of the Parties shall be responsible for any debts contracted after the signing of this Agreement unless both Parties have agreed to assume these debts.

15. Both Parties covenant that they shall willingly, at the request of either Party, or his or her successor or assigns, execute, deliver, and properly acknowledge whatever additional instruments may be required to carry out the intention of this Agreement, and shall execute, deliver, and properly acknowledge any deeds or other documents so that good and marketable title to any property can be conveyed by one Party free from any claim of the other Party.

16. This Agreement is entered into assuming that the Parties are to be married, and its effectiveness is expressly conditioned on the marriage between the Parties actually taking place. If, for any reason, the marriage is not consummated, the Agreement will be of no force or effect.

17. This Agreement contains the entire understanding of the Parties, and no representations or promises have been made except as contained in this Agreement.

18. If any term, provision, covenant, or condition of this Agreement is held by a court of competent jurisdiction to be invalid, void, or unenforceable, the remainder of the provisions shall remain in full force and effect and shall in no way be affected, impaired, or invalidated.

19. Each of the Parties by the execution of this Agreement intends that the provisions of this Agreement shall be binding on each of them and their heirs in the event of death, divorce, or a separation by and between the Parties.

20. Nothing in this Agreement shall affect the right of either Party voluntarily to transfer real or personal property to the other Party, or the right to receive property transferred by the other, during their lifetime.

21. Nothing in this Agreement shall affect the right of either Party to devise or bequeath property to the other Party in excess of that required by this Agreement. Nothing in this Agreement shall be construed as a waiver or renunciation of the right of either Party to take under the Last Will of the other.

22. The Parties and their respective heirs, devisees, legatees, personal representatives, guardians, successors in interest, and assigns shall be bound by the provisions of this Agreement.

23. Waiver of any breach of this Agreement does not constitute approval or waiver of subsequent breaches.

24. Amendments and modifications of this Agreement must be written and executed in the same manner as this Agreement.

25. This Agreement is to be governed by the laws of the State of

_____.

IN WITNESS WHEREOF, the Parties have executed this Agreement on the day and year first above written.

_____
JOHN SMITH

_____
JANE DOE

ACKNOWLEGMENT

STATE OF _____ :

                           ss

COUNTY OF _____ :

I certify that on this _____ day of _____, 19___, John Smith and Jane Doe, each personally appeared before me and severally acknowledged under oath, to my satisfaction, that they are the persons named in this Agreement and the persons who executed this Agreement, and that they each signed, sealed and delivered the same as each Party's act and deed for the purposes expressed in this Agreement.

_____
NOTARY PUBLIC

CERTIFICATION OF ATTORNEY

I hereby certify that I am an attorney at law, duly licensed and admitted to practice in the State of _____; that I have been retained by John Smith, a Party to this Agreement; that I have advised him with respect to the Agreement and explained to him the meaning and legal effect of it; and that Husband has acknowledged his full and complete understanding of this Agreement and its legal consequences, and has freely and voluntarily executed the Agreement in my presence.

_____, 19__   _____
                              Attorney for Husband

CERTIFICATION OF ATTORNEY

I hereby certify that I am an attorney at law, duly licensed and admitted to practice in the State of _____; that I have been retained by Jane Doe, a Party to this Agreement; that I have advised her with respect to the Agreement and explained to him the meaning and legal effect of it; and that Wife has acknowledged her full and complete understanding of this Agreement and its legal consequences, and has freely and voluntarily executed the Agreement in my presence.

_____, 19__   _____
                              Attorney for Wife

SAMPLE SCHEDULE A

	Value
Municipal bonds	$300,000
House and/or mortgage value: 43 Arnold Drive, Anytown, U.S.A.	350,000
Defined benefit plan	175,000
IRA	14,000
AT&T and derivative stock emanating from AT&T	167,000

	Value
Bank (cash on hand)	$ 27,000
Interest in Palm Beach home	275,000
(real estate venture)	46,000
Value of law practice	300,000
Personal insurance (whole life)	100,000
Interest in estate (Uncle David)	225,000
Checking account in ABC bank	6,000
Checking account in XYZ bank	17,000
Pension plan with prior company	65,000
Cash on hand	700
U.S. savings bonds	3,650
American Telephone and Telegraph	750
General Electric stock	12,000
Shore house	176,000

SAMPLE SCHEDULE B

House located at 305 Royal Court Anytown, U.S.A.	227,000
Interest in G.E. stock	75,000
Interest in mutual funds	123,000
Debts receivable	15,000
Money still in former husband's estate	175,000

	Value
Deferred annuity policy	$ 240,000
Personal jewelry	20,000
Stamp collection	69,000
401K plan	126,000
State pension plan	21,000
Bank account (American Bank)	6,483
Bank account (National Bank)	125

POSTNUPTIAL AGREEMENT FOR COMPLETE SETTLEMENT OF PROPERTY RIGHTS

The following form and paragraphs are most useful in creating a postnuptial agreement for the complete settlement of everything between the parties. Some of the paragraphs can, of course, be used in both and some are meant only for postnuptial agreements.

This type of agreement is generally utilized where the parties are already married and one of the spouses, for example, has recently completed a formal education or recently come into substantial funds that would elevate his or her financial situation in the future.

One of the important segments of this type of agreement is that just as in any other contract, there must be "consideration" between the parties. In this type of situation, the consideration for the agreement is generally a promise for a promise and must be so noted in the agreement.

POSTNUPTIAL AGREEMENT

Prepared by:_____(signature)
                    (typed name)

This Agreement is entered into on _____(date), between _____(name of husband) (Husband), and _____(name of wife) (Wife), collectively referred to as the "Parties." The Parties have lived together continuously as husband and wife since their marriage on _____(date), which took place in the City of _____, County of _____, State of _____. The Parties are currently residents of _____(State), now living at _____ _____(address), _____ County. This Agreement shall become effective as of _____(specify date).

ARTICLE 1. PURPOSES

Intent to Define Property Rights

1.01. It is the intention of the Parties to define and settle their respective and collective rights in the property owned separately by each of them or jointly by both of them, to determine and fix these respective and collective property rights in writing, and to avoid interests that they might acquire in the property of the other as incidents of their marriage relationship if it were not for the operation of this Agreement.

ARTICLE 2. RECITALS

Consideration

2.01. In recognition of the fact that _____(Husband or Wife) as of the effective date of this agreement will commence employment that will allow _____(him or her) to have the same opportunity to earn income and to acquire property as _____ (Wife or Husband), the Parties now recognize that it is in the best interests of both, and of their marital harmony, that each has the opportunity to acquire and manage his or her own separate property, free from any claim or interest of the other. This agreement is made in consideration of the

130

mutual rights to separate property created by it.

Husband's Separately Owned Property

2.02. Husband now owns as his separate property, notwithstanding the form of conveyance by which the property was taken or acquired, the following _____(real *or* personal *or* real and personal) property:_____

_____

(describe property, value, location, source, and date received).

Wife's Separately Owned Property

2.03. Wife now owns as her separate property, notwithstanding the form of conveyance by which the property was taken or acquired, the following _____(real *or* personal *or* real and personal) property:_____

_____

(describe property, value, location, source, and date received).

Property Held as Tenants by Entireties

2.04. Husband and Wife now own, as tenants by the entireties and not as tenants in common, the following_____ _____ (real *or* personal *or* real and personal) property: _____ _____*(describe property, value, location, source, and date received).*

Property Held as Tenants in Common

2.05. Husband and Wife now own, as tenants in common, the following _____(real *or* personal *or* real and personal) property:_____

_____

(describe property, value, location, source, and date received).

Marital Property

2.06. All other property other than that set forth in Paragraphs 2.02–2.05 of this Agreement owned or acquired by either party from the date of the marriage to the effective date of this Agreement is marital property.

Full and Complete Disclosure

2.07. This Agreement is entered into by Husband and Wife after full and complete disclosure by each party to the other of his or her assets, income, and property, and the assets, income, and property of his or her estate. To verify this full and complete disclosure, these exhibits are attached and incorporated to this Agreement: Exhibit A, listing the separate assets, income, and property of the Husband and his Estate; Exhibit B, listing the separate assets, income, and property of the Wife and her estate.

No Contemplation of Dissolution of Marriage

2.08. This Agreement is not made with any intention to obtain or in contemplation of a separation or divorce, or to effect a reconciliation between the Parties.

Representation by Independent Counsel

2.09. The Parties acknowledge that each party has been represented by independent counsel of his or her own choosing in the negotiation of this Agreement, and that each party has read the Agreement and has had the Agreement explained to him or her by counsel with respect to the meaning and legal consequences of the Agreement, and that each party fully understands the legal consequences of the Agreement, and enters into it freely and voluntarily.

ARTICLE 3. AGREEMENTS

Acknowledgment of Separate Property

3.01. Husband and Wife acknowledge and agree that the separate property listed in Paragraphs 2.02 and 2.03 of this Agreement is owned solely by the specified party free from any interest of the other that might otherwise arise because of the marital relationship.

Establishment of Separate Property

3.02. All income from and increases in value arising during marriage from the separate property of the Parties as set forth in Paragraphs 2.02 and 2.03 of this Agreement, regardless of the reason for the income or increase, shall be owned as the separate property of that party. All property that either party may acquire in the future during marriage by way of gift or inheritance, whether under a will or by intestate distribution, is similarly the separate property of the

132

owner-party. From the effective date of this Agreement, all wages, salary, and income of each party earned or received during marriage, together with all property purchased with such wages, salary, and income, shall also be the separate property of that party.

Treatment of Separate Property

3.03. Each party shall have the absolute and unrestricted right to manage, control, dispose of, or otherwise deal with his or her separate property as set forth in Paragraphs 2.02 and 2.03, or as created in Paragraph 3.02, free from any claim that may be made by the other party by reason of their marriage, and with the same effect as if no marriage had been consummated between them. By this Agreement, each party waives, discharges, and releases all right, title, and interest in and to the separate property of the other.

(Add if desired:)
Creation of Marital Property Fund

3.04. During the course of the marriage the Parties shall make equal periodic contributions to a fund for the maintenance of their household and the care and support of the children of the marriage. All property purchased with the proceeds of this fund shall be deemed marital property. Each party shall have equal rights in regard to the management of and disposition of all marital property.

Disposition of Property on Termination of Marriage

3.05. If the marriage should terminate for any reason other than the death of a party, and without regard to the fault of either party in causing the termination, all separate property as set forth in Paragraphs 2.02 and 2.03 and as established in Paragraph 3.02 of this Agreement shall remain the separate property of the respective Parties, and neither shall claim or have any right to compel the equitable distribution of any separate property. All marital property as set forth in Paragraph 2.06 of this Agreement and as created in Paragraph 3.04 of this Agreement shall be subject to a just and equitable distribution between the Parties.

Certain Property of the Husband
to Become Jointly Owned Property

3.06. The Parties agree that the following property, previously the separately owned property of Husband as described in Article 2 of this Agreement, shall become the jointly owned property of the Parties as _____(*specify, e.g.,* tenants in common): _____ *(describe property).*

Certain Property of the Wife
to Become Jointly Owned Property

3.07. The Parties agree that the following property, previously the separately owned property of Wife as described in Article 2 of this Agreement, shall become the jointly owned property of the Parties as _____(*specify, e.g.,* tenants in common): _____ *(describe property).*

Husband's Separate Property

3.08. The Parties agree that the following property, previously held by them as _____(tenants by the entireties *or* tenants in common) as described in Article 2 of this Agreement, shall become the separately owned property of the Husband: _____ _____ *(describe property).*

Wife's Separate Property

3.09. The Parties agree that the following property, previously held by them as _____(tenants by the entireties *or* tenants in common) as described in Article 2 of this Agreement, shall become the separately owned property of the Wife: _____ _____ *(describe property).*

Tenancy by the Entireties

3.10. The Parties agree that the following property, previously held _____(in the name of the Husband *or* in the name of the Wife *or* in the name of the Husband and Wife as tenants in common) as described in Article 2 of this Agreement, shall be owned by Husband and Wife as tenants by the entireties, and not as tenants in common, with the usual rights and incidents of that tenancy: _____
(describe property).

Tenancy in Common

3.11. The Parties agree that the following property, previously held _____(in the name of the Husband *or* in the name of the Wife *or* in the name of the Husband and Wife as tenants by the entireties) as described in Article 2 of this Agreement, shall be owned by the Husband and Wife as tenants in common with the usual rights and incidents of that tenancy: _____ *(describe property)*.

IN WITNESS WHEREOF, the Parties have executed this Agreement on the date first written above.

_____ *(signature)*
(typed name of husband)

_____ *(signature)*
(typed name of wife)

(Add acknowledgment and certification of attorneys here)

EXHIBIT A

Schedule of Assets, Property, and Income of _____ *(name of husband)* and his estate as of _____ *(date)*.

Assets	Value
_____	_____
_____	_____

Property	Value
_____	_____
_____	_____

Source of Income	Amount of Income
_____	_____
_____	_____

EXHIBIT B

Schedule of Assets, Income, and Property of _____ *(name of wife)* and her estate as of _____ *(date)*.
(See EXHIBIT A, above, for schedule form.)

MODIFICATION OF POSTNUPTIAL AGREEMENT

The following form and paragraphs are generally used to modify a postnuptial agreement. Certainly, it can be used to modify a prenuptial agreement. Although some people would advise you that these agreements can be changed orally, it certainly is the best practice to put any changes in writing.

MODIFICATION OF AGREEMENT

On _____ *(date)*, _____ *(name of husband)* (Husband) and _____ *(name of wife)*(Wife), collectively referred to as the "Parties," entered into _____(a prenuptial *or* a postnuptial) agreement (Agreement) concerning certain property and support issues related to their marriage. A copy of that Agreement is attached as Exhibit 1. The parties now desire to modify that Agreement. This agreement to modify the original Agreement (Modification Agreement) is entered into on _____*(date)*, to become effective as of_____ *(date)*.

Consideration

1. The consideration for the amendments to the Agreement described below shall be the mutual promises made in the Modification Agreement, and the new obligations created by it.

First Amendment

2. Paragraph _____ of the First Agreement is amended to read as follows: _____ *(set forth amended paragraph in full)*.

Second Amendment

3. Paragraph _____ of the First Agreement is deleted in its entirety.

Exhibits A and B Superceded

4. Exhibits A and B to the Agreement, in which the Parties set forth the full extent of their property and estate as of the time of execution of the Agreement, are superceded. New Exhibits A and B are attached to this Modification Agreement and incorporated by reference. Each reference in the Agreement to Exhibits A and B shall be deemed to refer to new Exhibits A and B as incorporated in this Modification Agreement, and not to original Exhibits A and B as incorporated in the Agreement.

Full Disclosure

5. Prior to entering into this Modification Agreement, both Parties have made to each other a full and complete disclosure of the

current nature, extent, and probable value of all their assets, income, property, estate, and expectancies.

First Agreement Otherwise Effective

6. Except as expressly amended in this Modification Agreement, the First Agreement shall continue in full force and effect.

IN WITNESS THEREOF, the Parties have executed this Agreement on the date first written above.

_____ *(signature)*
(typed name of husband)

_____ *(signature)*
(typed name of wife)

(Add acknowledgments, certification, and Exhibits A and B)

REVOCATION OF POSTNUPTIAL AGREEMENT

The following form and paragraphs are utilized by spouses to revoke a postnuptial agreement. This, of course, can be utilized to help institute a new postnuptial agreement due to changes in circumstance.

REVOCATION OF POSTNUPTIAL AGREEMENT

This Revocation Agreement was made and entered into on _____ *(date)*, by _____ *(name of husband)*, and _____ *(name of wife)*, collectively referred to as the "Parties."

On _____ *(date)*, the Parties entered into a postnuptial agreement, referred to as the "Agreement," a copy of which is attached as Exhibit 1.

The Parties now desire to terminate the Agreement; it is therefore agreed that the Agreement is revoked in all respects and for all purposes.

IN WITNESS WHEREOF, the Parties have executed this Agreement on the date first written above.

_____ *(signature)*
(typed name of husband)

_____ *(signature)*
(typed name of wife)

(Add acknowledgment and attorneys' certifications and copy of postnuptial agreement).

PROVISIONS FOR SUPPORT OF SPOUSES

TRANSFER OF PROPERTY TO SPOUSE AFTER MARRIAGE

The following form and paragraphs are a section that can be utilized to change ownership of certain property by either or both of the parties to the agreement. It can be utilized for both a postnuptial or a prenuptial agreement. The real purpose of the paragraphs allows people to take advantage of the marital gift tax deduction under the Internal Revenue Code. An attorney should be consulted concerning the applicability of this paragraph and its monetary importance.

IMMEDIATE TRANSFER ON MARRIAGE

Within thirty days after the date of their marriage, _____ *(transferor future spouse)* shall do the following:

(Select appropriate provisions:)

(a) _____ *(Name of transferor future spouse)* shall duly execute and deliver to _____ *(name of transferee future spouse)* a general warranty deed for real property situated at _____ *(address)* in the City of _____, State of _____. This property is more particularly described in Exhibit A attached to and incorporated into this Agreement for all purposes.

(b) _____ *(Name of transferor future spouse)* shall deliver to _____ *(name of transferee future spouse)* fully paid up policies on life insurance on _____ *(his or* her) life in a total amount of death benefit no less than $_____, and naming _____ *(name of transferee future spouse)* the irrevocable beneficiary and owner of all rights of these policies.

(c) _____ *(Name of transferor future spouse)* shall transfer to _____ *(name of transferee future spouse)* all of the securities listed in the schedule presented in Exhibit B attached to and incorporated into this Agreement for all purposes. These securities are to be free from all claims or liens.

(d) _____ *(Name of transferor future spouse)* shall pay to _____ *(name of transferee future spouse)* the sum of $_____.

(Attach Exhibits A and B.)

TRANSFER OF PROPERTY TO SPOUSE ON DEATH

The following form and paragraphs can be utilized in either a prenuptial or postnuptial agreement to change ownership of property, either real or personal, on the death of one of the parties. There are alternative forms presented for such use.

This form and these paragraphs create a contractual obligation, which is to take effect on the death of one of the parties. The purpose of this form and these paragraphs is to indicate clearly that making of a will will not obviate the need for this contract or obligation from one spouse to the other.

An attorney should be consulted concerning the state tax consequences of utilizing this idea or these paragraphs.

TRANSFER TO SPOUSE

_____ *(Name of transferor spouse)* (Decedent Spouse) agrees that if _____(he *or* she) is survived by _____ *(name of transferee spouse)* (Surviving Spouse) as Decedent Spouse's lawful _____(widow *or* widower), Surviving Spouse shall receive from Decedent Spouse's estate, free from all estate, inheritance, succession, or other death taxes,_____ _____ (the following property: _____ _____*[describe]* *or* the sum of $_____). This sum shall be paid to Surviving Spouse as soon after the death of Decedent Spouse as may be practicable, but in no event later than one year after_____ _____(his *or* her) death.

In the event that both spouses die simultaneously or under circumstances that make it impossible to determine the order of deaths, then the sum as promised above to Surviving Spouse shall be disposed of under the provisions of the Will of the Decedent Spouse.

(OR)

_____ *(Name of transferor future spouse)* (Decedent Spouse) agrees that if _____(he *or* she) is survived by _____ *(name of transferee future spouse)* (Surviving Spouse) as Decedent Spouse's lawful _____(widow *or* widower), Surviving Spouse shall receive from Decedent Spouse's estate, free of any estate, inheritance, succession, or other death taxes, the greater of (1) $_____ or (2) _____ percent of the "net estate" of Decedent Spouse. The "net estate" for purposes of this Agreement shall be the residue remaining in the estate after the deduction of all valid debts and funeral and administration expenses.

In the event that both spouses die simultaneously or under circumstances that make it impossible to determine the order of deaths, then the sum as promised above to Surviving Spouse shall be disposed of under the provisions of the Will of the Decedent Spouse.

(Continue with the following:)

In consideration for the above transfers, Surviving Spouse agrees to assert no interest other than as specified in this Paragraph in the estate of Decedent Spouse. Surviving Spouse specifically waives any

145

right to take an elective share against the Will of Decedent Spouse, or to take under the laws of intestacy.

This provision does not constitute a testamentary disposition, and this agreement is not intended as a Will. The rights and obligations created in this Paragraph shall remain in full force and effect regardless of the terms of any Will or Codicil, or provision revoking any Will or Codicil of Decedent Spouse.

ESTABLISHMENT OF TRUST FUND FOR SURVIVING SPOUSE

The following form and paragraphs can be utilized both in a prenuptial or a postnuptial agreement. It sets up a trust fund to be utilized by one of the parties after the death of the other for certain state tax consequences. An attorney should be consulted concerning whether this is useful or not for the parties.

The paragraphs are designed to allow the parties to take maximum advantage of the marital deduction by meeting certain requirements.

TRUST FUND

_____ *(Name of settlor-spouse)* agrees to create a valid trust by a testamentary disposition in the principal sum of $_____ in favor of _____ *(name of beneficiary-spouse), providing* _____ (he *or* she) is survived by _____ (her *or* him) as _____ (his wife *or* her husband), subject to the following terms and conditions:

(a) The entire net income from the trust shall be payable annually or in more frequent installments so long as _____ _____ *(name of beneficiary-spouse)* shall live.

(b) _____ *(Name of beneficiary-spouse)* shall have a general testamentary power of appointment exercisable alone and in all events to appoint the entire trust corpus either to _____ (his *or* her) estate or to any other person or persons, but in default of the exercise of this power the corpus shall pass in the manner designated in the Will of _____ *(name of settlor-spouse)*.

(c) No estate, succession, inheritance, or other death taxes imposed on the death of _____ *(name of settlor-spouse)* shall be paid from the income or corpus of the trust except to the extent that the assets of _____ (his *or* her) probate estate shall be insufficient to fully discharge all of these taxes.

In consideration for the above transfers, _____ _____ *(name of beneficiary-spouse)* agrees to assert no interest other than as specified in this Paragraph in the estate of _____ *(name of settlor-spouse)*. _____ _____ *(Name of beneficiary-spouse)* specifically waives any right to take an elective share against the Will of _____ *(name of settlor-spouse)* or to take under the laws of intestacy.

Although this provision requires that _____ *(name of settlor-spouse)* makes a specific testamentary disposition, the provision itself does not constitute a testamentary disposition, and this agreement is not intended as a Will. The rights and obligations created in this Paragraph shall remain in full force and effect regardless of the terms of any Will or Codicil, or provision revoking any Will or Codicil of Decedent Spouse.

ANNUITY TO SPOUSE PAYABLE DURING MARRIAGE

This form and paragraphs can be utilized in both a prenuptial and postnuptial agreement. The purpose is to provide a party the guaranteed sum of money on a regular basis. It is used in lieu of transferring property or providing for a lump sum payment at a future time.

This particular segment may be exceedingly complicated and technical because it concerns taxation; a tax attorney should be consulted if the reader desires to utilize it.

ANNUITY

It is agreed that _____*(name of donor-spouse)* shall pay, or shall purchase an annuity contract sufficient to pay, to _____*(name of donee-spouse)* during _____ (their marriage *or* his life *or* her life) the sum of $_____ per month, or so much of that amount as _____ *(name of donee-spouse)* may desire for _____(his *or* her) sole and individual use as _____(he *or* she) may see fit, without the necessity of accounting for these payments to anyone.

It is understood between the Parties that this provision will in no way affect the Parties' legal duty of support during their marriage, and that the payments due under this provision are to be in addition to, not in lieu of, any amounts paid in the satisfaction of that duty. If the marriage of the Parties terminates for any reason other than the death of a party, _____ (all annuity payments to _____ *[name of donee-spouse]* shall terminate *or* these annuity payments shall continue as a full and complete discharge of the duty of _____*[name of donor-spouse]*, and shall be in lieu of alimony, spousal support, or any other payments made in discharge of the duty of continued support).

ANNUITY PAYABLE TO SURVIVING SPOUSE

The following form and paragraphs are another way of providing for future income for one of the parties. Tax consequences concerning this type of transfer are also exceedingly important and a tax attorney should be consulted.

ANNUITY

In the event that _____ *(name of donor-spouse)* (Donor) dies during the marriage, _____ *(name of donee-spouse)* (Donee) shall receive an annuity of $_____ per year for so long as _____(he *or* she) shall be payable _____ *(specify method of payment, e.g.,* in equal quarterly installments). Donor shall purchase during _____(his *or* her) life, a commercial annuity for these payments from any solvent insurance company.

This provision does not constitute a testamentary disposition, and this agreement is not intended as a Will. The rights and obligations created in this Paragraph shall remain in full force and effect regardless of the terms of any Will or Codicil, or provision revoking any Will or Codicil of _____ *(name of donor-spouse).*

(Add if desired:)

In consideration for the above payments, _____ *(name of donee-spouse)* agrees to assert no interest in the estate of _____ *(name of donor-spouse).* _____ *(name of donee-spouse)* specifically waives any right to take an elective share against the Will of _____ *(name of donor-spouse)* or to take under the laws of intestacy.

AGREEMENT TO OBTAIN LIFE INSURANCE

This form and paragraphs are utilized by parties to require life insurance to be obtained by one of the parties for the benefit of the other. This type of provision can be utilized in lieu of transfer of property, in lieu of annuities, or in lieu of subsequent payments.

A tax attorney should be consulted about the ownership of the policy that might be purchased. There are different tax consequences depending on whether the husband, wife, or estate of either owns the policy.

LIFE INSURANCE

_____ *(Name of donor-spouse)* (Donor) agrees that _____(he *or* she) will obtain, if insurable at standard rates, policies of _____*(type of insurance, e.g., whole life)* insurance on _____(his *or* her) life in the face amount of $_____, within ____ *(number)* days after the marriage of the Parties, and shall designate _____ *(name of donee-spouse)* (Donee) as the irrevocable primary beneficiary of the policies. The Donor further agrees to continue making payments of the insurance premiums in order to maintain the policies in full force and effect as long as the Parties remain married.

(Optional)

The Donor further agrees to transfer ownership of the policy to Donee, within _____ days after the marriage of the Parties, and to retain no incidents of ownership or benefits in the policy or its proceeds after the date of the transfer.

(Optional)

The Donor further agrees that the proceeds payable to the Donee on Donor's death shall be free from all estate, inheritance, succession, or any other death tax, and Donor agrees to provide for this in _____(his *or* her) Will.

(Optional)

In consideration for the above insurance,_____ _____ *(name of donee-spouse)* agrees to assert no interest in the estate of _____ *(name of donor-spouse)*. _____ *(name of donee-spouse)* specifically waives any right to take an elective share against the Will of _____ *(name of donor-spouse)* or to take under the laws of intestacy.

AGREEMENT TO CHANGE LIFE INSURANCE BENEFICIARY

The following form and paragraphs are generally utilized in a prenuptial agreement concerning the naming of one party by the other as the irrevocable beneficiary of a life insurance policy already in existence. Once again, a tax attorney should be consulted due to significant potential tax consequences.

CHANGE OF LIFE INSURANCE BENEFICIARY

_____*(Name of donor-spouse)* agrees that
_____ (on the day of *or* within) _____ *(number)* of days
after their marriage _____(he *or* she) shall arrange for
_____ *(name of donee-spouse)* to be desig-
nated as the irrevocable primary beneficiary of the following life
insurance policies: _____
_____*(specify names of insurance
companies, policy numbers, types of policies, and the face amount of
each).*

(Optional)

In consideration for the above designation,_____
_____ *(name of donee-spouse)* agrees to
assert no interest in the estate of_____
_____*(name of donor-spouse).* _____
_____*(name of donee-spouse)* specifically
waives any right to take an elective share against the Will of
_____*(name of donor-spouse)* or to take
under the laws of intestacy.

AGREEMENT TO MAKE DEVISE

The following form and paragraphs are generally utilized in an antenuptial agreement where the parties have agreed to require certain obligations in the Will of the other.

DEVISE

_____ *(Name of devisor-spouse)* (Devisor) covenants and agrees that on marriage, _____(he *or* she) will make a provision in _____(his *or* her) last Will and Testament that _____ *(specify, e.g.,* the sum of $_____) be devised to _____ *(name of devisee-spouse)* (Devisee) as soon after Devisor's death as may be practicable if the Devisee survives Devisor as _____(his *or* her) lawful _____(widow *or* widower).

Although this provision requires that Devisor make a specific testamentary disposition, the provision itself does not constitute a testamentary disposition, and this agreement is not intended as a Will. The rights and obligations created in this Paragraph shall remain in full force and effect regardless of the terms of any Will or Codicil, or provision revoking any Will or Codicil of Devisor.

PROVISION SPECIFYING STANDARD OF LIVING FOR AWARD OF ALIMONY

The following provisions concern themselves with fixing alimony through the agreement, as opposed to later on when tempers might flare.

STANDARD FOR AWARD OF ALIMONY

If the marriage should terminate for any reason other than the death of one of the parties, and regardless of fault of either party in causing the termination, either party may seek continued support from the other in the form of alimony, spousal support, or other payments or transfers of property for the purpose of providing support. However, in determining the amount of any award or payment, the appropriate standard to be applied shall be the standard of living of the party to be supported before the marriage and not the standard of living enjoyed during the marriage.

PROVISIONS FOR CARE OF CHILDREN

PROVISION FOR SUPPORT OF MINOR CHILDREN BY FORMER MARRIAGE

The following form and paragraphs are generally utilized for providing for the support of the child or children of the other party. There are, of course, numerous alternatives to this and all should be explored openly with the other party.

SUPPORT OF MINORS

(First Alternative:)

_____*(Name of future husband)*, during the existence of the forthcoming marriage, agrees to provide a home and reasonable support for the care and maintenance of_____
_____*(name of children)*, the minor children of Wife by a former marriage, until they attain the age of _____years. In the event of the death of Wife during the existence of the marriage, this obligation shall continue in full force and effect until the children attain this age.

_____*(Name of future wife)*, during the existence of the forthcoming marriage, agrees to provide a home and reasonable support for the care and maintenance of_____
_____*(names of children)*, the minor children of Husband by a former marriage, until they attain the age of____ years. In the event of the death of Husband during the existence of the marriage, this obligation shall continue in full force and effect until the children attain this age.

(Second Alternative:)

Wife shall be under no duty or obligation to provide a home or support for _____*(name of children)*, the minor children of Husband by a former marriage. However, in the event of the death or inability of Husband to support these children, Wife agrees to provide a home and reasonable support for their care and maintenance until they reach the age of____ years. This obligation shall continue in full force and effect during the existence of the forthcoming marriage, and after the death of Husband, until the children attain this age.

Husband shall be under no duty or obligation to provide a home or support for _____*(name of children)*, the minor children of Wife by a former marriage. However, in the event of the death or inability of Wife to support these children, Husband agrees to provide a home and reasonable support for their care and maintenance until they reach the age of____ years. This obligation shall continue in full force and effect during the existence of the forthcoming marriage, and after the death of Wife, until the children attain this age.

ADOPTION OF CHILDREN OF PROSPECTIVE SPOUSE

The following form and paragraphs usually concern themselves with the prenuptial agreement in which one of the parties agrees to adopt the child or children of the other. This, of course, can be utilized in a postnuptial agreement also.

ADOPTION

_____ *(Name of future husband)* agrees to legally adopt _____ *(names and ages of children)*, the minor children of Wife, as his own, and agrees that they shall have the same right of inheritance in his property at his death as if they were his natural children.

_____ *(Name of future wife)* agrees to legally adopt _____ *(names and ages of children)*, the minor children of Husband, as her own, and agrees that they shall have the same right of inheritance in her property at her death as if they were her natural children.

PROVISION FOR MINOR STEPCHILD ON DEATH OF NATURAL PARENT

The following form and paragraph is used in a prenuptial agreement only when the potential new stepparent does not adopt the minor child of the other but makes provisions nonetheless. It can be used in a postnuptial agreement also.

PROVISION FOR MINOR STEPCHILD

If _____ *(name of spouse who is natural parent)* should die during the marriage of the Parties and any of _____(his *or* her) children of a prior marriage are under the age of _____ years, _____ *(name of other spouse)* shall within one month after the death _____*(specify, e.g.,* pay a sum of $_____ in cash to the testamentary guardian of the children) as designated in the Will of _____ _____ *(name of spouse who is natural parent),* or, if there is no Will, to the guardian appointed in the matter.

PROVISION FOR NATURAL CHILD ON DEATH OF PARENT

The following form and paragraphs are generally utilized where one of the parties has had children by his or her prior marriage and the prior partner has died. In addition, substantial assets were accumulated by this person and he or she wishes to make sure that his or her children receive the entire benefit.

This form and paragraphs can be utilized in both prenuptial and postnuptial agreements.

CHILDREN OF FORMER MARRIAGE

_____ *(Name)*, in order to provide for
_____(his *or* her) children by a former marriage, shall leave the
sum of $_____, which represents the value of the property
accumulated during _____(his *or* her) former marriage, to
_____(his *or* her) children by that marriage. The sum shall be
distributed as follows:

To _____ *(name of child)*, $_____.
To _____ *(name of child)*, $_____.
To _____ *(name of child)*, $_____.

If any child who is to receive a devise under the terms of this
Paragraph should die without spouse or issue, that child's share shall
be divided among the survivors of the children who are to receive
devises under this Paragraph, or the survivor's heirs by right of
representation.

On payment of the above mentioned amounts, _____
_____ *(name of other spouse)* shall be entitled to take
all of the remaining property of_____*(name)*,
subject to prior payments of all debts, costs of administration, and
expenses of the last illness and funeral.

Although this provision requires that _____ *(name)*
make a specific testamentary disposition, the provision itself does not
constitute a testamentary disposition, and this agreement is not
intended as a Will. The rights and obligations created in this
Paragraph shall remain in full force and effect as long as the Parties
are married, regardless of the terms of any Will or Codicil, or
provision revoking any Will or Codicil of_____*(name)*.
The termination of the marriage for reason other than the death of
either party shall serve to revoke this Paragraph.

PROPERTY OF SPOUSE TO DESCEND TO CHILDREN OF FORMER MARRIAGE

The following form and agreement can be utilized by both prenuptial and postnuptial agreements where both parties wish to protect their natural children.

TESTAMENTARY DISPOSITION OF PREMARITAL PROPERTY

At the death of either party, his or her separate property acquired prior to the date of the marriage as set forth in_____

_____(*specify e.g.*, Exhibits A and B of this Agreement), together with all income and proceeds from, increases in value of, and other property acquired in exchange for any such separate property, shall pass to his or her children or their heirs free from any claim from the other party, whether based on a right to take an elective share against a Will, a right under the law of intestacy, or any other right created by law or custom.

Although this provision establishes the right of each party to make a specific testamentary disposition, the provision itself does not constitute a testamentary disposition, and this agreement is not intended as a Will.

SPECIAL PURPOSE CLAUSES

POSTNUPTIAL RATIFICATION OF ORAL PRENUPTIAL AGREEMENT

This form and paragraph is utilized by parties both for prenuptial and postnuptial agreements to affirm and ratify any prior oral agreement. It is always recommended, to prevent any present or future misunderstandings, that all agreements be in written form.

RATIFICATION

The Parties to this Agreement affirm that the Agreement was orally made and entered into prior to their marriage, and each party, by his or her signature below, ratifies every covenant and agreement in this Agreement as if this document had been prepared and executed prior to the marriage of the Parties.

SECRET ANNEX TO PRENUPTIAL AGREEMENT

This form and paragraph may be utilized as certain sections of a prenuptial or postnuptial agreement in states where agreements should be filed in the county or the state. This can help maintain privacy of the individuals and of the agreement.

ANNEX TO PRENUPTIAL AGREEMENT

Recitals

This is an annex to the Prenuptial Agreement made and entered into on _____ (*date*), by Husband (Husband), and Wife (Wife), both collectively referred to as the "Parties."

Certain terms of the Agreement are set forth in Exhibit A, which is attached and incorporated by reference. However, the Parties prefer that the remaining terms of their Agreement not be made public.

Now, therefore, the Parties agree that the remaining terms of their prenuptial agreement are as follows: _____ (*set forth terms*).

(Attach Exhibit A.)

LEGISLATION

LEGISLATION

The following is a copy of the Uniform Premarital Agreement Act, which has been proposed to all of the states. As of this writing a small number of states have actually accepted the general idea. This law uses the term "premarital agreement," which is intended to replace the term "antenuptial agreement" and "prenuptial agreement." This law, as adopted by each state legislature, is likely to be changed slightly.

UNIFORM PREMARITAL AGREEMENT ACT

Section

---

1.   Definitions:

As used in this Act:

(1) "Premarital agreement" means an agreement between prospective spouses made in contemplation of marriage and to be effective upon marriage.

(2) "Property" means an interest, present or future, legal or equitable, vested or contingent, in real or personal property, including income and earnings.

2.   Formalities

A premarital agreement must be in writing and signed by both parties. It is enforceable without consideration.

3.   Content

(a) Parties to a premarital agreement may contract with respect to:

(1) the rights and obligations of each of the parties in any of the property of either or both of them whenever and wherever acquired or located;

(2) the right to buy, sell, use, transfer, exchange, abandon, lease, consume, expend, assign, create a security interest

in, mortgage, encumber, dispose of, or otherwise manage and control property;

(3) the disposition of property upon separation, marital dissolution, death, or the occurrence or nonoccurrence of any other event;

(4) the modification or elimination of spousal support;

(5) the making of a will, trust, or other arrangement to carry out the provisions of the agreement;

(6) the ownership rights in and disposition of the death benefit from a life insurance policy;

(7) the choice of law governing the construction of the agreement; and

(8) any other matter, including their personal rights and obligations, not in violation of public policy or a statute imposing a criminal penalty.

(b) The right of a child to support may not be adversely affected by a premarital agreement.

4. Effect on Marriage

A premarital agreement becomes effective upon marriage.

5. Amendment, Revocation

After marriage, a premarital agreement may be amended or revoked only by a written agreement signed by the parties. The amended agreement or the revocation is enforceable without consideration.

6. Enforcement

(a) A premarital agreement is not enforceable if the party against whom enforcement is sought proves that:

(1) that party did not execute the agreement voluntarily; or

(2) the agreement was unconscionable when it was executed and, before execution of the agreement, that party:

(i) was not provided a fair and reasonable disclosure of the property or financial obligations of the other party;

(ii) did not voluntarily and expressly waive, in writing, any right to disclosure of the property or financial obligations of the other party beyond the disclosure provided; and

(iii) did not have, or reasonably could not have had, an adequate knowledge of the property or financial obligations of the other party.

(b) If a provision of a premarital agreement modifies or eliminates spousal support and that modification or elimination causes one party to the agreement to be eligible for support under a program of public assistance at the time of separation or marital dissolution, a court, notwithstanding the terms of the agreement, may require the other party to provide support to the extent necessary to avoid that eligibility.

(c) An issue of unconscionability of a premarital agreement shall be decided by the court as a matter of law.

7.   Enforcement: Void Marriage

If a marriage is determined to be void, an agreement that would otherwise have been a premarital agreement is enforceable only to the extent necessary to avoid an inequitable result.

8.   Limitation of Actions

Any statute of limitations applicable to an action asserting a claim for relief under a premarital agreement is tolled during the marriage of the parties to the agreement. However, equitable defenses limiting the time for enforcement, including laches and estoppel, are available to either party.

9.   Application and Construction

This [Act] shall be applied and construed to effectuate its general purpose to make uniform the law with respect to the subject of the [Act] among states enacting it.

10. Short Title

This [Act] may be cited as the Uniform Premarital Agreement Act.

11. Severability

If any provision of this [Act] or its application to any person or circumstance is held invalid, the invalidity does not affect other provisions or applications of this [Act] which can be given effect without the invalid provision or application, and to this end the provisions of this [Act] are severable.

12. Time of Taking Effect

This [Act] takes effect _____ and applies to any premarital agreement executed on or after that date.

13. Repeal

The following acts and parts of acts are repealed:
(a)
(b)
(c)

LEGAL SERVICES AGREEMENT

LEGAL SERVICES AGREEMENT

THIS AGREEMENT, dated the _____ day of _____, 19___, is made between John J. Client, whose address is 43 Arnold Drive, Anytown, USA, hereinafter referred to as "Client" and David A. Saltman, Esq., whose address is P.O. Box 1438, East Windsor, New Jersey 08520, hereinafter referred to as "Law Firm."

1. Legal Services to be Provided.

You agree that the Law Firm will represent you in compilation of a Prenuptial Agreement between you and Fannie Gertrude. The legal work includes all of the necessary research, investigation, correspondence, preparation, and drafting of the Prenuptial Agreement and all other legal conferences in person, by telephone, etc., with you and with others and work related to properly representing you in this matter.

2. Legal Fees.

The Law Firm cannot predict or guarantee what your final bill will be. This will depend on the time spent on your agreement and on other expenses.

    A. Minimum Fee. The Client agrees to pay a minimum fee of $750.00 for legal services regardless of the amount of time actually spent on this agreement.

    B. Hourly Rate. The Client agrees to pay the Law Firm for legal services at the following rate:

Rate Per Hour	Services of
$150.00	David A. Saltman, Esq.

    C. All Services Will Be Billed. You will be billed at the hourly rate set forth in the paragraph above for all services rendered. This includes telephone calls, dictating and reviewing letters, travel time to and from meetings, legal research, negotiations, and any other services related to this matter.

    D. The Law Firm may require that experts be retained directly by you. You will be solely responsible to pay the experts.

3. Bills.

The Law Firm will send you itemized bills from time to time. You will be charged interest at a yearly rate of 18 percent on any balance due that is not paid within 30 days from the date of the bill.

4. Your Responsibility

You must fully cooperate with the Law Firm and provide all information relevant to the issues involved in this matter. You must also pay all bills as required by this Agreement. If you do not comply with these requirements, the Law Firm may ask the Court for permission to withdraw from representing you. The Law Firm will also withdraw at your request.

5. No Guarantee

The Law Firm agrees to provide conscientious, competent, and diligent services and at all times will seek to achieve solutions that are just and reasonable for you. However, because of the uncertainty of legal proceedings, the interpretations and changes in the law proceedings, the interpretation and changes in the law, and many unknown factors, attorneys cannot and do not warrant, predict, or guarantee results or the final outcome of any case.

Signatures.

Client and Law Firm have read and agree to this Agreement. The Law Firm has answered all of the Client's questions and fully explained this Agreement to Client's complete satisfaction. Client has been given a copy of this Agreement.

Law Firm: Client:

By:_____   _____
    DAVID A. SALTMAN, ESQ.   JOHN J. CLIENT

GLOSSARY

Acknowledgment A declaration by a person who has signed a document that such a signature is a voluntary act, made before a duly authorized person, such as a notary public or attorney.

Administrator A court-appointed person or entity who takes care of the estate of a person who dies without a will.

Administrator expenses The expenses allowed to the person administering or taking care of an estate of the deceased. Generally these include postage and commissions for sales of property.

Administratrix Female administrator.

Adopt To take as one's own, i.e., take a child as one's own. When you adopt a child, the law in most states sees no difference between an adopted child and a biological child once the adoption is completed. See Natural parent.

Against a will Occurs when a state allows a spouse to take more from the estate of the deceased spouse than the deceased left in the will. For example, in New Jersey, if there is one child and the will leaves everything to that child, the spouse can take up to a total of 50 percent of the estate. This allows the child to take only 50 percent of the estate. A good reason for a prenuptial agreement. See Will.

Alimony What you agree to pay for the support of your former spouse after you are divorced. Some states call this "maintenance."

Amendment A change in an agreement.

Annulment A determination by the courts that the marriage entered into was fraudulent and never took place.

Antenuptial agreement A written mutual agreement regarding the division of assets made before marriage should a permanent separation or divorce occur. It is the same as a premarital or prenuptial agreement.

Asset(s) Both real and personal property. Anything of value, be it art, real estate, stamps, cash, or anything else. Also includes intrinsic value.

Attest To affirm as true, to be witness to by signing a document.

Attorney certification The attestation or certification by an attorney that a signature or statement is correct.

Beneficiary The person(s) who receive benefits or assets or income from an estate or from a contract or insurance policy.

Bequeath To give personal property through a will.

Bequest A gift of personal property by a will.

Case law The law as interpreted by the judges of a state or by the Supreme Court of the United States.

Certification Acknowledgment by either an attorney or notary public that something is true, accurate, and authentic.

Certified copy A copy of a court or public document that would indicate something is, in fact, actual and/or true.

Civil law That segment of the law dealing with contractual matters rather than criminal.

Codicil An addition to a person's last will and testament. It's usually cheaper and easier to add a codicil than to redo the will.

Coercion To do something involuntarily or to be forced to do something.

Cohabitation To be cohabiting with someone, usually of the opposite sex.

Community property distribution Community property, a system of property ownership used in certain western states. See Equitable distribution.

Consideration Something of value given in exchange for performance when a contract is being made. Usually a promise or an object of value, such as money.

Construction An interpretation of ambiguous parts of a statute.

Contingency fee An attorney's fee that is dependent upon the outcome of the litigation.

Corpus The body or substance of an estate; the monies involved.

Counsel An attorney, a legal adviser.

Court A tribunal that administers justice according to federal, state, or common law.

Covenant An agreement between parties that something will be done or that something is true.

Curtesy The right of a husband to his deceased wife's property regardless of the provisions of the will.

Death taxes Estate taxes generally imposed either by the state or the federal government or both to tax the estate of the deceased.

Decedent spouse The spouse who has died.

Deed A written instrument that conveys ownership of real property.

Devise A gift of real, and sometimes personal, property.

Disclaimer A denial or refusal of legal claim.

Distributive share The portion of an estate that is going to a particular individual.

Divorce The termination of a marriage by the courts through the powers given to them by the state. Divorces are obtained in different ways in different states. Some states now use the term "dissolution of marriage."

Divorce a mensa et thoro A rare type of judgment by a court that ends the right of cohabitation between the parties but leaves the persons married, i.e., a partial divorce.

Divorce a vincuolo matrimonii A divorce by the courts because of marital misconduct.

Domicile The principal place of residence.

Donor spouse One giving the property, i.e., life insurance, houses.

Dower right The right of interest that the wife or child has to a deceased husband's or father's real property. See Curtesy.

Elective share The share of an estate that a spouse chooses to take.

Emancipation The age at which one can take care of oneself, either eighteen or twenty-one, depending on the individual state. See Lawful age.

Enforce To carry out laws.

Enjoin To legally stop someone from doing something by means of an injunction.

Equitable distribution The equitable, but not necessarily equal, division of property acquired during the marriage. Defined according to state law. See Community property distribution.

Estate All that a person owns, whether real or personal property.

Estate tax Tax based on value of property left by the deceased. See Death taxes.

Execute To sign a contract.

Executor The person who is designated by the deceased to carry out the terms of a will.

Executory To be executed in time, i.e., not yet fully signed.

Executrix A female executor.

Failure of consideration In a contract, failure to give something in exchange for a promise of money.

Fiduciary The person entrusted with the care of another person, or for a trust or an estate.

Flat fees A single amount of money that an attorney quotes for service, regardless of the amount of hours involved.

General warranty deed A deed that claims there are no liens or judgments against the property and promises to protect the guarantee.

Gift A voluntary transfer of property from one person to another without any consideration or compensation.

Guardian A court-appointed person who looks after the welfare of an incompetent person.

Heir The person who inherits or is entitled to receive something in the event of another person's death.

Hourly fee A rate of pay an attorney charges based on the amount of time spent in performance of a service.

Household goods Personal property found on the premises. Does not include the house itself, anything attached to it permanently, or the land itself.

Incapacity An inability to enter into a contract either because of age or because of mental inabilities.

Independent counsel An attorney who has been hired to look out for your interests only.

Inheritance The property passed by the decedent to someone by means of a will.

Inter vivos While the parties to transaction are living, rather than upon death.

Intestate Having died without a will. Property usually goes to the state if there are no heirs.

Irrevocable beneficiary The person who benefits from one's will, estate, or insurance policy without one being able to change it.

Jointly owned property Property owned together.

Joint tenancy Property held by two or more persons equally. When one of them dies, then the other owns the property without its passing through the estate.

Jurisdiction The power to hear a case; also the legal entity, such as a court or state that makes legal determinations.

Law The body of rules of conduct either through case law, statutes, or other regulations that govern our day to day activities.

Lawful age Either eighteen or twenty-one, depending on the state. At the time you reach lawful age, you are considered an adult and able to exercise certain rights. See Emancipation, Minor.

Laws of intestacy Laws of the individual states that govern how property is distributed when there is no will.

Leasehold The interest or estate in which a tenant holds a lease.

Lien A claim somebody has in your property for security of the payment of a debt, judgment, mortgage, or taxes.

Life estate The right someone gives you to use something or to derive the benefits from for the rest of your life.

Lis pendens A public notification that you are involved in a lawsuit about a piece of real property.

Majority The legal age, i.e., eighteen or twenty-one.

Marketable title A clear title; property that does not have any liens or encumbrances on it.

Minor A child under the age of either eighteen or twenty-one, depending on the individual state.

Modification of agreement An amendment or change in an agreement.

Mortgage A lien on real estate that is security for repayment of a loan.

Mortgagee The entity, usually a bank, that has lent money to a property owner and holds a mortgage as security for repayment of the loan.

Mortgagor The property owner who is repaying the mortgage loan.

Mutual revocation An agreement to revoke an agreement.

Mutual wills Generally, a will executed by two people (married or divorced) that declares each person will leave equal portions of their estate to their spouse and equal portions to other persons or entities, such as their children or different charities.

Natural parent The biological parent.

Net estate The amount of money or value left in an estate after all the taxes and debts have been paid.

Notary public A person who can attest to the genuineness and authenticity of signatures at the end of documents.

Parties The persons involved in a contract or litigation, i.e., the husband and the wife.

Pendente lite See Lis pendens.

Personal property (Personalty) That which is not real estate. Property that is movable, not attached to the land.

Postnuptial agreement An agreement entered into between the parties much like a prenuptial agreement but done after the marriage commences.

Power of attorney An instrument authorizing one person to act on behalf of another, usually in signing legal documents and in making legal decisions.

Premarital property Any and all property, whether it be real or personal, acquired before marriage.

Real property Real estate, i.e., property that is not personal property. Generally refers to land, houses, and their permanent attachments.

Residency The location of home(s).

Residue Whatever is leftover in the estate after everything else has been paid off, including the beneficiaries.

Revocation The nullification of a segment, portion, or all of an agreement.

Revocation agreement An agreement between the parties to nullify all or part of an agreement.

Rights of inheritance The right of a person to inherit from a parent or some other family member under the individual state laws.

Securities Stocks and bonds owned by a person.

Separate property The property that is not owned by both of the parties but owned individually.

Separately owned property See Separate property.

Spousal support Pendente lite support, alimony, or designated support made through an agreement or by the courts to support one of the parties.

Spouse The husband or wife in a marriage.

Statute The law as enacted in a particular state or by the federal government.

Statutory That which is designated by statute. See Statute.

Stepchild The son or daughter of a spouse who has remarried.

Support See Spousal support.

Surviving spouse The spouse who has not died.

Survivorship The right of ownership that a surviving joint tenant has to the other's property upon death. Prevents the heirs from making claim to the property.

Tenancy The right of possession of real property by ownership or by tenancy.

Tenancy at sufferance The right to live in a place until you are asked to leave.

Tenancy at will The right to possess real property until the landlord or tenant decides the property shall be vacated.

Tenants in common The ownership of real property that, upon the death of a partner, passes to the deceased's heirs, not to the partner.

Testament The disposition of real or personal property.

Testamentary capacity The legal ability to make a will.

Testate Having made a valid will.

Testator The person who makes a will.

Testatrix A woman who makes a will.

Testimony A statement given under oath.

Trust An arrangement or entity set up to hold or protect assets for a third person.

Vested A fixed interest in something.

Vested interest See Vested.

Vested remainder A right to something that is leftover, usually in an estate.

Waive To forgo rights, claims, or privileges.

Waiver See Waive.

Will A declaration of how a person wants to dispose of property upon death.

INDEX